What Real Alaskans

EAT

Not Your Ordinary Cookbook

J. Stephen Lay

Illustrations by Barbara Santora

EPICENTER PRESS

Alaska Book Adventures™

Epicenter Press is a regional press founded in Alaska whose interests include but are not limited to the arts, history, environment, and diverse cultures and lifestyles of the Pacific Northwest and high latitudes. We seek both the traditional and innovative in publishing nonfiction books, and contemporary art and photography gift books.

Publisher: Kent Sturgis
Acquisitions Editor: Lael Morgan
Illustrations: Barbara Santora
Cover and book design: Newman Design
Proofreader: Sherrill Carlson
Printer: Haagen Printing
Bindery: Lincoln & Allen

Library of Congress Control Number 2003112519
ISBN 0-9724944-3-X

Booksellers: This title is available from major wholesalers. Retail discounts are available from our trade distributor, Graphic Arts Center Publishing Co., PO Box 10306, Portland, OR 97210. Phone 800-452-3032.

PRINTED IN THE UNITED STATES OF AMERICA

First Edition
First Printing, October 2003

10 9 8 7 6 5 4 3 2 1

To order single copies of WHAT REAL ALASKANS EAT, mail $12.95 plus $4.95 for shipping (WA residents add $1.55 state sales tax) to: Epicenter Press, PO Box 82368, Kenmore, WA 98028.

Discover exciting ALASKA BOOK ADVENTURES!
Visit our online Alaska bookstore at **www.EpicenterPress.com**, or call our 24-hour, toll-free hotline at 800-950-6663. Visit our online gallery featuring the artist of dog mushing, Jon Van Zyle at **www.JonVanZyle.com**.

Dedication

I thank my parents for my culinary education. My mother was an excellent cook and through example she taught me food was supposed to taste good. In our small southern Illinois town, she was considered a kitchen radical because she used so many spices and seasonings. Some of her exotic recipes required as much as a half-teaspoon of "white pepper!" Remember this was the 1950s and ketchup was considered extreme.

My father—again, through example—motivated my desire to learn to cook. When I was eleven, my mother injured her knee and was hospitalized for several weeks. After she returned home, she used crutches for most of the next year and couldn't get around to prepare the complete meals we ate twice a day.

Into this culinary vacuum stepped my father, who took over all cooking duties.

After three days I realized three things. One, my father didn't know his way around the kitchen. Two, he wasn't going to improve. Three, while I didn't know much about cooking, I could learn. And I did.

All of that was 42 years and about 150 pounds ago.

So, I dedicate this book to my mother, Bennye B. Lay, for educating me about food, and to my father, Willard C. Lay, for encouraging my first attempts.

Preface

Oh, by the way...

You may notice that I haven't given serving guidelines for how many people each recipe feeds. There is a perfectly valid reason. I don't know. The best answer is, it depends. Who are you serving?

Most of these recipes will feed 24 to 30 supermodels for a week. With the exception of the "World's Best Brussels Sprouts Recipe," four to six American eaters should finish most at one sitting. (Don't get me going on brussels sprouts!)

This rule of thumb will not apply if you're an Alaskan, it's been 50 below zero for a week, the car won't start, you're almost out of firewood, and the electricity is flickering on and off. In that case, the receipe might feed two or three of you.

Ignore everything I said if you're feeding a teenager. If you have a teenager at the table, double the recipe. Keep in mind that young moose is more tasty and tender, but a large moose feeds more people. Even a teenager will have trouble finishing a moose in one sitting.

Table of Contents

Vegetables 35

Meat 64

Fish 82

Desserts and Sweets ... 114

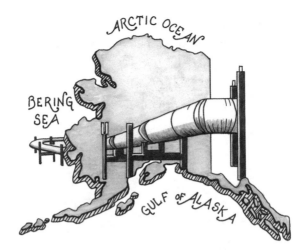

Introduction
Alaskans & Food

Food is serious business in the North.

The original residents lived entirely off the land—hunting, gathering, and fishing. Out of necessity, the first Russians who came to Alaska in the 1700s relied heavily on local foods, but they also introduced agriculture to the land and attempted to grow grain and vegetables, generally with poor results. One of the reasons the Russians established Fort Ross in California was to grow food for their northern holdings. Eventually they sold their California colony to John Sutter and the rest is history.

The Russians found they couldn't grow much in the North, but they did harvest and export one of Alaska's most common commodities. They had a prosperous ice business. Russians cut winter ice from a lake in Sitka, packed it in sawdust, and shipped it to San Francisco.

After the U.S. government bought Alaska from Russia in 1867, few Americans made their way north until the great gold rushes at the turn of the century. Food was literally a matter of life and death for the men and women who trekked to the North seeking their fortunes. In its *Tribune Extra Klondike* edition of 1898, *The Chicago Daily Tribune* advised each stampeder to take with them:

200 lbs. bacon,
300 lbs. flour,
25 lbs. dried peaches,
25 lbs. dried apples,
25 lbs. dried apricots,
25 lbs. pitted prunes,
25 lbs. coffee,
10 lbs. tea,
50 lbs. sugar,

150 lbs. beans,
90 lbs. oatmeal,
25 lbs. cornmeal,
100 lbs. rice,
5 lbs. baking powder,
5 lbs. yeast,
5 lbs. soda, and
One large box of matches

In 1898, the food supply for a year, which weighed in at 1,200 pounds including shipping boxes, cost about $90. Stampeders needed it. C. W. Adams joined of thousands of gold-seekers stampeding to the gold fields. In his memoir, *A Cheechako Goes to the Klondike,* he remembered the Northwest Mounted Police, who patrolled the Alaska-Canada border and collected customs duties on everything entering Canada, barring entry to anyone with less than "1,100 pounds of grub." By all accounts, this policy saved many lives.

Food was sold in Dawson, but at unaffordable prices— $3 a pound for butter or a dozen eggs, $16 for a gallon of milk, $1.50 each for oranges and apples. Martha Black, who walked the trail in 1898, could not afford to supplement her own supplies at local prices. "How I longed for a change of diet—some fruit and vegetables!" Instead, she "gulped down the ever-unpalatable cornmeal mush, prunes, and tea with no milk or sugar."

The *Tribune* also advised carrying a rifle and one hundred rounds of .30-.30 brass shell cartridges, a large hunting knife, and an assortment of fishing tackle. It correctly assumed the intrepid "Argonauts," as the Klondike stampeders called themselves, would shoot or hook additional food. Many Alaskans today continue to rely on hunting and fishing to feed their families.

Many in the "Lower 48," also known as the "puny states," or "Outside," are surprised to learn how dedicated Alaskans are to their gardens during the short but sunny summers. They never plant just one zucchini plant, which are prolific under the midnight sun. One plant provides squash for personal use, and the second is to give away. Planting zucchini means people know you have your own and won't give them to you. But grocery bags overflowing with the little green squash still mysteriously appear on your doorstep when you aren't home.

Alaskans love a good trophy. Where else do people celebrate one hundred pound cabbages? But they plant for the dinner table with more than coleslaw in mind. Broccoli, peas, carrots, cauliflower, beans, squash, spinach, potatoes, and turnips also are among the most popular vegetables.

With the completion of the Alaska Railroad in 1923, freight costs fell, and perishable items such as the oranges and bananas became available year-round.

Alaskan recipes and menus can more or less be divided into pre-pipeline and post-pipeline. Pre-pipeline relied heavily on concentrated, easy-to-store foods. During the winter, few fresh vegetables appeared on the menu. In the larger cities, air transport brought in out-of-season fruits and vegetables, but they were expensive and purchased only for special occasions. Many older Alaskans treasure special family memories of oranges or other fruit for Christmas or a birthday.

Most pre-pipeline Alaskans used powdered milk with Milkman being the favored brand. Even those who bought real milk mixed it 50-50 with powdered. Many Alaskans who came of age in the pre-pipeline days don't care for fresh tomatoes, because—except for cherry tomato varieties—they don't grow well in the north, and store tomatoes just don't compare to the real thing. Neither of my daughters, born in Sitka and raised in Fairbanks, will eat tomatoes.

Post-pipeline menus are more adventurous. One of the after-effects of the pipeline, and there were many, was increased air service and more retail competition. Today's menus may include almost anything. Recently I was served a salad of "free range greens accented with cilantro-basted salmon in pecan crust." Doesn't "free range greens" mean they grew wild? Isn't that a weed? Does it make sense to fly weeds to Alaska? If you want to serve weeds, at least pick them locally. Please excuse my digression.

Most of the recipes in this cookbook are pre-pipeline. I won't claim that I invented them, because I didn't. They were given to me, and I made personal adjustments to adapt to my family's tastes. Or, to be honest, sometimes I used what I had in the refrigerator that night, and it worked. I did develop a few recipes of my own, which are identified. Other recipes date from before western contact, but I think those will be obvious. They are also the only ones I have not made and served my family, but I have tasted them.

Enjoy.

Drinks

Caffeine and alcohol historically fueled the North, and they continue to do so today. Russians preferred tea for their caffeine and drank large quantities of it imported from China, paying for it with sea otter furs and other pelts. They also brewed teas from local plants. Labrador tea, from a short plant growing on the muskeg, makes an acceptable substitute for fuller bodied teas.

Miners kept coffee on the stove all day long. By all accounts it was strong and usually diluted with canned milk—when available—and lots of sugar.

Alcohol was one of the first products made in Alaska. The Russians made home brews, and the Americans followed suit. During the gold rushes, Fairbanks and Nome had local breweries. Today's Alaska brand beer, brewed in Juneau, uses a recipe discovered in the state archives from an earlier Juneau brewery.

During the early American era, saloons provided camaraderie and stiff drinks. Whisky was the most common drink because it packed a lot of wallop in small amounts, a critical advantage due to high transportation costs. But the saloons stocked a range of alcoholic beverages for the thirsty drinker willing to pay for something different. Martha Black reported men paying $30 a pint for champagne in the dance halls of Dawson during the first winter of the Klondike Gold Rush.

Prohibition closed the Alaska Territory's breweries, but it did nothing to reduce demand. Bootleggers imported Canadian booze or made their own. Many bootleggers knew the coast better than officers enforcing the law and sped through rocky waters at high speed to elude their pursuers. Such rocky patches of ocean are still called "rum runner rocks."

Home brewing and wine making are common hobbies fulfilling two needs—an indoor activity and booze. Tales abound of homemade booze and its aftermath. Not all would-be brewers and distillers are successful. Most of the stories relate to failures and accidents. In my first and only attempt to make wine, I used salmonberries, a relative of the raspberry. My do-it-yourself brewing book specified that more sugar resulted in stronger wine, and yes, I used the maximum. California wineries need not worry; my salmonberry wine never threatened their livelihood. It tasted like equal parts of vodka and vinegar.

Cranberry Liqueur

Add a little class to your liquor cabinet.

---

12 cups cranberries

4 cups pure grain alcohol. Less potent vodka may be substituted.

3-4 cups water

5-7 cups sugar

1. Crush cranberries and refrigerate overnight in a stainless steel or ceramic crock.

2. Add alcohol and let stand, covered, for another twenty-four hours or more.

3. Boil two cups of water with five cups of sugar for five minutes to make syrup.

4. Cool to room temperature.

5. Strain the cranberry-alcohol mixture.

6. Mix cranberry-alcohol mixture into sugar syrup.

7. Taste. If it is too tart, make another syrup using one cup of water and one or two cups of sugar. If alcohol level is too strong, dilute with water. If the liqueur needs additional "punch," add alcohol or a mixture of alcohol and water.

8. Bottle.

Labrador Tea

You're going to have to pick your own tea out in the muskeg. Pick only the smaller leaves, and pick in the spring. Leaves are fresher with more flavor, and there are fewer mosquitoes in the muskeg that time of year. Wear insect repellent. For the bigger mosquitoes use a 12-gauge shotgun but shoot to kill. Wounded, they get mad.

6-12 dried Labrador tea leaves
2 cups hot water
Add honey or sugar to taste

1. Steep tea leaves in boiling water for five minutes.
2. Strain.
3. Sweeten to taste.

Spruce Tea

Originally spruce tea was an Athabascan medicine, and it was not sweetened. It has a medicine taste but with sweetening, the taste improves.

Handful spruce needles
1-2 cups water
Add honey or sugar to taste

1. Boil spruce needles in water.
2. Strain.
3. Sweeten to taste.

Rosehip Tea

Wholesome, healthy and despite that, damn good.

---

    1 tea bag
    2 cups boiling water
    1 tablespoon dried rosehips
    3 or 4 whole cloves
    Add honey or sugar to taste

1. Steep tea bag, rose hips, and cloves in boiling water for five minutes.

2. Strain.

3. Sweeten to taste.

Cold-Fighting Hot Chocolate

Experiment with flavored brandies—particularly coffee-flavored. Dark rum gives a fuller flavor than light rum.

---

2 packages instant hot chocolate mix
Hot water
Rum or brandy
Whipped cream or ice cream (optional)

1. Prepare the hot chocolate using only three-quarters of the water called for in the instructions.

2. Add enough rum or brandy to replace the missing water.

3. Top with whipped cream or ice cream.

4. Enjoy fighting the cold. More than two of these and you'll fight it in bed, sound asleep.

Hot Toddy

Use any alcohol, but the most commonly used are whisky, rum, and brandy.

---

1 jigger alcohol—your choice
1 jigger hot water
1 teaspoon sugar

1. Combine sugar and alcohol in a tumbler.

2. Add hot water.

Cold Toddy

Historically, despite the abundance of ice, few Alaskans used ice in their drinks.

---

  1 jigger alcohol—your choice
  1 jigger water
  1 teaspoon sugar

1. Combine sugar and alcohol in a tumbler.

2. Add water and an ice cube or two.

Champagne Cocktail

Champagne cocktails were popular at turn-of-the-century celebrations such as New Year's Eve. For the record, that is turn of the century 1900—not 2000. Surprisingly, the mining towns consumed a lot of champagne.

  Cold champagne
  1-2 dashes of bitters
  ¼ peel of one lemon
  ½ teaspoon sugar
  Ice

1. Put bitters, lemon peel and sugar in a 10-12 oz. tumbler.

2. Half fill tumbler with ice.

3. Top with champagne.

Bread

Today you can buy almost any kind of bread found anywhere in the world, but the traditional breads of the North are those brought first by the Russians and later by the gold seekers. Black breads fed the Russians on a daily basis with special treats for special occasions such as their Easter bread. Quick breads—biscuits, hardtack, and pancakes—fueled the American prospectors when they came to the North.

As communities were established, bakeries opened, providing breads, sweets, and pies. Ma Pullen, one of the richest women in Skagway during the 1898 gold rush, made her first fortune baking pies and selling them to hungry stampeders. Arriving in Skagway broke, she sold her goods from a tent. Some stampeders changed their minds about going to the gold fields and converted their supply of flour into doughnuts, which they sold for money to pay their way back home from Dyea and Skagway.

Men comprised most of the early populations, and they did their own cooking. They had limited utensils, and many had never cooked before. For the most part, they made simple breads with limited choices of ingredients. Biscuits, sourdough, and pancakes replaced Russian dark breads after the Americans took over.

Americans were frugal with their leftovers. During the Depression, two brothers living in a cabin below the Alaska Agricultural College and School of Mines in the "Flats" or "Yertchville" near Fairbanks were notorious for their sauerkraut and pancake sandwiches. The brothers were known too for a perpetual pot of stew on the back of their stove. As it emptied, they continuously refilled it with whatever meat or vegetables were available. They were among the dozens of single men who wanted an education, but couldn't afford the $55 a month for room and board on campus. Today their alma mater is the University of Alaska Fairbanks.

Supplies brought into Alaska were expensive, and residents quickly learned to adjust and substitute local supplies for imported. Bear fat makes an excellent replacement for lard in biscuits. To some, it is even better than lard or shortening. Bear fat biscuits, according to one of my friends, are "flakier than my last two girlfriends." I don't know if I agree. The biscuits are excellent, but I also knew both girlfriends.

Potato Oatmeal Muffins

Like all muffins, resist the temptation to mix more than enough to combine

1 cup rolled oats

1 cup milk

2 cups flour

1 cup sugar

2 tablespoons baking powder

1 teaspoon baking soda

1 teaspoon salt

1 teaspoon cinnamon

¼ teaspoon nutmeg

½ cup butter, melted

2 eggs, slightly beaten

2 teaspoons vanilla

1¼ cups mashed potato

1. Combine oats and milk; set aside.

2. In a large bowl combine flour, sugar, baking powder, baking soda, salt, cinnamon, and nutmeg.

3. Add melted butter, eggs, vanilla, and potatoes to the oats/milk mixture.

4. Thoroughly mix.

5. Add wet ingredients to dry ingredients and stir only until moistened. Important: Do not over-mix.

6. Fill greased muffin cups three-quarters full.

7. Bake at 375 degrees for 18-20 minutes.

Rhubarb Muffins (or loaves)

You've grown the rhubarb; now you have to use it. Fortunately, it is good, and this is a very good way to use it. Taste the finished muffins before adding the topping. If they are not sweet enough, double up on the topping. Personally I skip the topping because I like the tart-sweet flavor of the muffin.

2 cups flour

1 teaspoon baking soda

½ teaspoon salt

1¼ cups brown sugar, packed

½ cup oil

1 egg

1 cup buttermilk

1 teaspoon vanilla

2 cups rhubarb, chopped

Topping:

½ cup brown sugar, packed

1 tablespoon butter, melted

½ teaspoon cinnamon

1. Combine flour, soda, and salt.

2. In a separate bowl, blend sugar with oil.

3. Whisk in egg, buttermilk, and vanilla.

4. Add rhubarb.

5. Stir into dry ingredients until flour is moist.

6. Spoon into greased or paper-lined muffin tins, filling three-fourths full, or spoon into two greased bread loaf pans.

7. Mix topping ingredients and sprinkle over batter.

8. Bake at 350 degrees for 20-25 minutes for muffins, 40-45 minutes for loaves, or until cake tester comes out clean.

9. Let cool in pans 10 minutes before removing.

Hoe Cake

Hoe cake recipes come in dozens of variations. This is the most basic I've found. They were easy to prepare and used commonly available ingredients. They were a common food throughout the nation's frontier exploration period. When the first Americans came to Alaska with their cornmeal and salt pork, they brought hoe cakes with them.

---

2 cups cornmeal
1 teaspoon salt
1 cup boiling water
¼ cup bacon drippings

1. Mix cornmeal and salt.

2. Slowly pour meal into boiling water, constantly stirring.

3. Mix until thick and let cool.

4. Divide into eight equal parts and flatten each piece into a flat cake about three inches across.

5. Fry in bacon drippings using medium to medium-high heat for about 5 minutes on each side or until golden brown.

Gingerbread

This may seem to be an odd selection, but in reading old diaries, newspaper clippings, and books, I've found several references to making gingerbread in the camp for special occasions.

This is a slightly modified recipe I took from my grandmother's handwritten cookbook. She never made it to Alaska. She wanted to join the Klondike Gold Rush of 1898, but didn't. My father was born on December 30, 1898. According to my family's oral history, she didn't want to climb the trail when she was pregnant.

4 cups flour

¼ cup lard or shortening

¼ cup butter

½ cup molasses

2 tablespoons milk*

1 teaspoon ginger, powdered

½ teaspoon baking soda

½ teaspoon salt

½ teaspoon cream of tartar

*If the batter is too thick, add more milk.

1. Mix flour with salt, baking soda, ginger, and cream of tartar.

2. Cut lard and butter into flour mixture.

3. Combine molasses and milk.

4. Add liquids to dry ingredients.

5. Pour into greased pan and bake 325-350 degrees for 20-30 minutes.

Doughnuts

Doughnuts were another popular gold rush treat. They were working hard and didn't worry about calories.

3½ to 4½ cups flour
1 tablespoon baking powder
1 teaspoon salt
2 eggs
2 tablespoons butter, lard, or shortening, melted
1 cup sugar
1 cup canned milk (or fresh milk)
Lard, shortening, or oil for frying
Sugar for topping

1. Combine and mix 3½ cups of flour, baking powder, and salt.

2. Lightly beat the eggs.

3. Mix sugar and melted butter into eggs.

4. Add about ⅓ of the flour mixture and mix into the egg mixture.

5. Stir in ⅓ cup of milk and thoroughly mix.

6. Repeat steps four and five until all milk and flour mixture is incorporated into the dough.

7. Let the dough rest for at least 30 minutes in the refrigerator.

8. After the dough has rested, flour a surface and roll dough out to about ½-inch thickness.

9. Cut as many doughnuts as possible.

10. Do not re-roll scraps. The doughnuts will be tough.

11. Fry in at least 3 inches of melted shortening or oil at 375 degrees.

12. Cook for about 3 minutes on each side.

13. Do not try to cook too many at one time, or they will become greasy.

14. Fry the holes and scrap pieces. The holes and smaller scraps may cook a little faster; larger pieces may require an extra minute or two.

15. Remove when done and drain on paper towels turning after a minute or two.

16. Sprinkle tops with sugar, and serve.

Note: Add cinnamon or other flavorings to sugar sprinkle.

Zucchini Bread

If you plant zucchini, learn to make this bread. It is tasty, freezes well, and uses a lot of zucchini—not quite as many as your plants will yield, but a lot.

---

2 cups flour
1 cup whole-wheat flour
2 teaspoons baking powder
1 teaspoon ground cinnamon
½ teaspoon baking soda
½ teaspoon salt
2 eggs
1 cup brown sugar, packed
1 cup milk
½ cup unsweetened applesauce
2 teaspoons vanilla extract
2 cups zucchini, shredded

1. Preheat oven to 350 degrees.

2. In large bowl, mix flours, baking powder, cinnamon, baking soda, and salt.

3. In small bowl, lightly beat eggs.

4. Stir in sugar, milk, applesauce, and vanilla until blended.

5. Add zucchini.

6. Combine with dry ingredients and stir just until blended.

7. Grease 9- by 5-inch loaf pan.

8. Pour batter into prepared pan.

9. Bake 1 hour or until tester inserted into center comes out clean.

10. Cool for 10 minutes before removing from pan.

Bear Fat Biscuits

Use black bear fat instead of grizzly bear fat. But whichever you use, never use a "stream bear"—a bear that has been eating salmon. Fish gives the fat a "distinctive" flavor.

---

2 cups flour
1 teaspoon baking powder
½ teaspoon cream of tartar
¼ teaspoon salt
1-2 tablespoons sugar
½ cup rendered bear fat (or shortening)
⅔ cup milk condensed (or fresh milk)

1. Preheat oven to 450 degrees.

2. Thoroughly mix dry ingredients together.

3. Cut in bear fat or shortening until thoroughly incorporated with the dry ingredients.

4. Add milk and mix enough so that the dough holds together.

5. Mix, using your hands, to eliminate dry spots in dough.

6. Roll out to about ½-inch thickness on a floured surface.

7. Cut into biscuits.

8. Make a shallow thumbprint in the middle of each biscuit.

9. Bake for 10-12 minutes. When done, biscuits will be golden brown.

Sourdough Starter

Sourdough has to be kept alive. Many miners carried a pouch around their neck with the sourdough in it. Their body heat kept it alive. It was that precious. Today, there are many sourdough starter recipes. You can find dried sourdough starters in some grocery stores and gift shops. True sourdough, however is from the wild and each has its own distinctive flavor.

---

3 cups flour
1 package yeast
2½ cups warm water

1. Mix flour and yeast together in large glass or ceramic bowl.

2. Make a well in the center of the flour-yeast mixture.

3. Pour water into well.

4. Mix the ingredients together.

5. Cover with a towel and set in a warm, draft-free spot.

6. Wait for 24 hours.

7. If bubbly, you have sourdough; if not, throw it away and start over.

Note: Keep sourdough starter in a glass jar with a tight lid in your refrigerator until needed.

Sourdough Bread

This makes a great crusty loaf. Because of the differences in different starters, the water is a guess. Make relatively stiff dough.

---

3 cups sourdough starter
½ cup sugar
½ cup melted shortening or cooking oil
1½ to 2 cups water
6½ to 7½ cups flour
1-2 teaspoons salt

1. Mix flour, sugar, and salt together.

2. Stir in starter, shortening, and water.

3. Thoroughly blend.

4. On a well-floured surface, knead for 10 minutes or so.

5. Pull off about 2 cups of dough and put into a glass jar to replenish your starter.

6. Roll remaining dough into a large ball.

7. Place in a large lightly oiled bowl, cover, and allow to rise 8-10 hours.

8. Divide into two loaves.

9. Lightly oil two bread pans and put loaves in them.

10. Cover and allow to rise 2-4 hours.

11. Bake in a 325-degree pre-heated oven 55-60 minutes.

Sourdough Pancakes

This was the ultimate food of the isolated miner. Easy to make, quick, and it didn't take too much fuel.

---

4 cups sourdough starter
2 cups lukewarm water
2½ cups flour
2 eggs
4 tablespoons oil or melted butter
¼ cup evaporated milk (or fresh milk)
1 teaspoon baking soda
2 tablespoons sugar

1. The night before, thoroughly mix starter, water and flour together.

2. Cover with towel and let sit out overnight in warm, draft-free place.

3. Remove 1 cup of dough and save for future sourdough recipes.

4. Stir in the eggs, oil, milk, soda, and sugar. Mix just enough to blend together.

5. Set aside for 15 minutes or more.

6. Heat frying pan or griddle until a drop of water evaporates quickly.

7. Grease griddle before cooking each batch of pancakes.

8. Cook pancakes 3-5 minutes, until bubbles pop on the sides.

9. Flip and cook on other side.

10. Serve immediately.

Blueberry Sourdough Pancakes

Use sourdough pancake recipe and mix one cup of fresh blueberries into batter before cooking.

Quick, Fake, Last-Minute, Sort-of-Sourdough-Tasting Pancakes

Use packaged pancake mix such as Bisquick. Follow instructions but replace the water with pilsner-type beer. Use only real beer; light beers don't have enough flavor to substitute for sourdough. This isn't real sourdough, but it works when you don't have time to make them from scratch. Anyone who knows real sourdough will be offended, but tourists and relatives visiting from the Lower 48 will rant and rave how much they like your sourdough, and it's a lot less work.

Blueberry Muffins

If you gather your blueberries along the coast, remember to soak them overnight in salt water to get the worms out. Or skip it. You're cooking the berries and a few worms add protein. It doesn't affect the flavor. Berries from the Interior don't need the soak.

2 cups flour
2 teaspoons baking powder
½ teaspoon salt
1 teaspoon vanilla
¼ cup shortening
2 eggs, slightly beaten
1 cup sugar
½ cup milk
2 cups blueberries*

You may substitute red huckleberries or cranberries for the blueberries. Or, use half red berries and half blue.

1. Mix together the flour, salt, and baking powder.

2. Mix the vanilla, shortening, eggs, and sugar.

3. Stir in half the flour mixture into the vanilla-shortening-egg-sugar mixture.

4. Stir in half the milk.

5. Stir in the remaining flour mixture.

6. Stir in the remaining milk.

7. Add the blueberries.

8. Bake in muffin tin for 25 minutes at 350 degrees.

Vegetables

New residents who have grown up in the smaller states find Alaska vegetables a contradiction. The locally grown veggies rival anything they've ever encountered. They're good, and they're big. Newcomers never encountered Alaska prices either. In 1971, during my first week in Alaska, I needed celery for something I was making. (This story makes a lot more sense if you know we arrived nearly broke and, after paying the first month's rent and deposit, we were down to the penny jar until my first paycheck.) Celery in Sitka's Lakeside Grocery was forty-nine cents. I thought that was outrageous. It was just nine cents in Fredericksburg, Texas, just two weeks before.

At that price, I decided I was going to get the biggest stalk, and went through the entire bin weighing every one. At the checkout, I discovered Alaska stores sold celery by the pound. I paid $2.16 for the biggest damn celery in the store, and we had exactly forty-six cents to last until Friday.* Naturally I bought the celery on Tuesday.**

It wasn't until I started growing my own celery several years later that I actually enjoyed the stuff again. But celery, like most vegetables grown in the land of the midnight sun, is a treat. It's not bland chewy supermarket stuff; it's a zingy, crunchy vegetable worth eating alone. Our carrots are almost too sweet. I don't ever remember picking enough peas from the garden for a meal, because my daughters grabbed them off the vine for snacks.

Even the family dogs munched in the garden. Toshie, our Scottish terrier, became addicted to green bell peppers. He stood on his hind legs and snagged them off the plant. I had to plant peppers outside the fence to save any for the table. OK, I was a softie—I put a few plants inside the fence so Toshie could have some. Besides, he was fun to watch as he snuck up to the plant and cautiously looked over his shoulder to make sure no one saw him before he grabbed a pepper. Then he would run to one of his hiding places to eat his trophy. And, yes, he actually ate them.

During the summers, residents enjoy their fresh veggies, but traditionally they relied on bulk and canned foods that can be stored for the nine months when nothing grows. Root crops such as potatoes, carrots, and turnips joined cabbage and dried beans in dominating most pre-pipeline menus.

On Thursday we found $1.07 in the couch.

**We didn't starve. Alaskans are generous people, and a commercial fisherman I met the day before gave me a small salmon as a "welcome to Alaska" gift. It was delicious—particularly with sautéed celery. He didn't know that I needed the fish. It was entirely a friendly gesture on his part.*

Stir-Fried Barley

The result is similar to fried rice. And like fried rice, ingredients often depend on what's on hand. Like fried rice, this can be a meal or side dish. Add left-over meat and make it a main dish.

---

1 cup pearl barley, uncooked
1 tablespoon oil
1 tablespoon sesame seed oil
2-3 cloves of garlic, peeled and sliced lengthwise
½ cup chopped onion
½ cup chopped carrots
½ cup chopped celery
1 cup fresh or defrosted frozen green peas
Salt and pepper to taste

1. Cook the barley according to the instructions on the package, but use 10% less water than called for. You want the barley cooked, but "dry," not mushy.

2. When barley is cooked, drain in a colander while cutting veggies.

3. Heat oils in wok until smoking.

4. Add garlic, onion, carrots, and celery. Stir-fry until slightly limp, 2-4 minutes.

5. Add barley and stir-fry, while mixing barley and vegetables, 2-4 minutes.

6. Add green peas and stir-fry while mixing all ingredients together, 2-4 minutes.

7. Serve hot.

Beef Borscht

Borscht came with the Russians, and, as every Russian knows, beets are the basis for many wonderful soups. Forget your prejudices against beets and enjoy.

---

2 lbs. beef brisket
1 lb. beets, peeled and sliced thin
2 onions, medium, peeled and sliced thin
1 tablespoon sugar
1 clove garlic, minced
1 tablespoon lemon juice
Salt and pepper to taste

1. Cover beef with water in a large pot.

2. Bring to a boil and reduce heat to simmer for 90 minutes.

3. Skim foam from top.

4. Add lemon juice, onions, beets, sugar, and garlic to broth.

5. Cook until meat is tender, 2-3 hours.

6. Remove meat and shred into bite-sized chunks.

7. Taste and correct seasonings.

8. Serve hot.

Hearty Beet Soup

Sort of another borscht since it uses beets as a key ingredient. Of course it is also sort of another vegetable soup.

---

1 cup navy beans, dry (or three 16-oz. cans drained)
2½ lbs. beef or moose meat
½ lb. bacon, chopped
10 cups water
1 bay leaf
8-10 peppercorns
2 cloves garlic
2 tablespoons dried parsley
1 carrot
1 celery stalk
1 onion
8-10 beets for soup
2 cups cabbage, shredded
3 potatoes, cut into ¾-inch chunks
One 29-oz. can tomatoes
1 tablespoon tomato paste
¼ cup red wine vinegar
¼ cup sugar
1 lb. kielbasa or similar sausage
Sour cream

1. Cover beans with water and soak for at least 4 hours.

2. Drain beans and, in a large pot with a lid, add beans, cover with water, and bring to a boil.

3. Reduce heat to simmer and cook until beans are tender.

4. Drain; set aside.

5. Combine moose, bacon, and water in large soup pot; bring to a boil; reduce heat to simmer and cover.

6. After 45 minutes, skim fat from surface.

7. Add bay leaf, peppercorns, garlic, parsley, carrot, celery, and onion.

8. Cover and simmer over low heat for about 90 minutes.

9. In a separate pot, cook beets in boiling water until tender, about 45 minutes.

10. Drain and discard water.

11. Peel and cut each beet into one-half inch chunks.

12. Add beets, cabbage, potatoes, tomatoes, tomato paste, vinegar, and sugar to beef and bacon. Bring to a boil and simmer 45 minutes.

13. Cut kielbasa into chunks and add with navy beans to soup. Simmer 20 minutes more.

14. Garnish with a dollop of sour cream before serving.

Brussels Sprouts

This is my favorite recipe for Brussels sprouts. But it takes planning and lots of advanced preparation. In the spring, plant a large plot with just Brussels sprouts so you will have plenty. Surround it with a fence to keep out the moose, but plant cabbages and additional sprouts along the perimeter of the fence. The moose will eat them, but they can't get inside the fence to get your sprouts. All summer, water, fertilize, and weed the entire plot.

The night before the opening day of hunting season, take the fence down. Get up early the next morning and shoot a moose. Enjoy fresh moose meat.

I hate Brussels sprouts! Have you ever seen how they grow? They are little clusters of leaves growing under other leaves on a long thick stalk. I mean… do you want to eat anything that grows in a plant's armpit?

Sauerkraut

This isn't the wimpy school lunch stuff. Good home-made kraut packs real flavor.

---

10 lbs. green cabbage, as fresh as possible
½ cup pickling salt

1. Thoroughly wash cabbage; throw away bruised or damaged leaves.

2. Quarter and cut away the core and discard.

3. Shred the cabbage into uniformly fine pieces.

4. Into a large non-metallic container (earthenware crock is best) put half the cabbage and sprinkle with half the salt.

5. Mix the cabbage and salt.

6. Let stand for 5-10 minutes; juices will begin to come out of the cabbage.

7. Save juices and repeat steps, four, five and six with remaining cabbage and salt.

8. Pack all cabbage into crock.

9. Cover cabbage with juice.

10. It must be covered by juices to prevent spoilage.

11. If you do not have enough juice to cover, make additional brine using 4 tablespoons salt to 2 quarts water.

12. It is vital keep cabbage submerged during fermentation.

13. Cover tub securely with plastic.

14. Store at 65-75 degrees, and don't disturb for at least three weeks.

15. After three weeks, remove plastic wrap. There should be no bubbles of CO_2 gas. If there are, recover and check again in 2-3 days.

16. Finished sauerkraut should appear with no white spots or unpleasant odors. Texture should be firm.

17. Pack finished sauerkraut into clean jars and store in refrigerator for up to six months.

Sautéed Cabbage

I prefer to serve this hot and throw away the leftovers. I don't like leftover cooked cabbage

---

1 head cabbage (red or green), shredded
1 apple, cored and chopped
1 onion, sliced or chopped
2-4 slices bacon, thick sliced and heavy smoked
1-3 teaspoons vinegar
1-3 teaspoons sugar
Salt and pepper to taste

1. Fry bacon until crisp using medium heat. Crumble when cooled.

2. Sauté the chopped onion in the bacon grease for 3-5 minutes.

3. Add cabbage, apple, and bacon.

4. Barely cover cabbage with water.

5. Cook uncovered at medium heat until soft, 10-12 minutes.

6. Season to taste with vinegar and sugar. Most prefer about equal amounts of vinegar and sugar.

Cabbage and Beet Soup

Many Alaskans ate some version of this soup as a late winter or early spring meal. Everything except the lemon juice came from a can or the cold bin. If no lemons were left, the cook probably used a bit of vinegar, or nothing, because nine months after harvest the beets lose most of their sweetness.

---

1 medium cabbage, coarsely sliced

1 lb. beets, sliced

2-3 carrots, sliced

1 onion, sliced

3 cloves garlic, minced

6-10 peppercorns

2 bay leaves

2 stalks celery, sliced into 1-inch pieces

3 lb. soup bones

1 lb. stew meat

¼ cup lemon juice

One 29-oz. can tomatoes

Salt and pepper to taste

1. Put meat and bones into a 12-quart stockpot.

2. Add canned tomatoes and enough water to cover plus an inch.

3. Bring to a boil.

4. Boil for 30 minutes.

5. Skim the froth that rises to the top.

6. Add beets, carrots, celery, onions, peppercorns, cabbage, garlic, and bay leaves.

7. Reduce heat to a simmer and partially cover.

8. Simmer until vegetables are soft and cooked, about 90 minutes.

9. Remove bones, pick off meat, and return it to the pot. Discard the bones.

10. Remove bay leaves, add lemon juice, and serve hot.

Shredded Carrot and Beet Salad

This is absolutely beautiful, and people who taste it will love it, beets and all. Chopped dried apples instead of raisins are also good.

---

3 carrots, peeled
¼ cup raisins
3 beets, peeled
Dressing:
½ cup vegetable oil
¼ cup red-wine vinegar
1-3 teaspoons sugar
½ teaspoon dry mustard
Salt and pepper to taste

1. Shred carrots and place them in a small bowl.

2. Mix in raisins.

3. Shred beets and place in another small bowl.

4. Combine oil, vinegar, sugar, mustard, and salt.

5. Cover and shake until well mixed.

6. Split the dressing in half and pour over vegetables.

7. Toss to coat.

8. Cover and refrigerate for at least 15 minutes.

9. Combine carrot-raisin and beets and serve cold.

Cranberry Carrots

This gives you a sweet-sour carrot dish. It is perfect for last-minute potlucks. If you are more adventurous, try using the canned whole cranberry sauce. This dish is a quick last minute dish that adds to any meal from informal to very stuffy.

---

1 lb. carrots, cut into thin coins
One 16-oz. can of cranberry sauce
Salt and pepper to taste

1. Boil carrots in lightly salted water until tender-crisp, about 5 minutes.

2. Drain and immediately stir in cranberry sauce, thoroughly coating.

3. Serve.

Midnight Sun Cabbage

Don't make this one in advance. Cook it, and serve immediately.

---

4 tablespoons oil
½ medium head red cabbage, shredded
½ medium head green cabbage, shredded
1 medium green bell pepper, cut into strips
1 medium yellow bell pepper, cut into strips
2 ribs celery, sliced ½ inch thick
2 medium carrots, cut into ¼-inch coins
1 large onion, sliced in ¼-inch slices
1 cup rhubarb cooking sauce (See page 56.)
Salt and pepper to taste

1. Heat oil until smoky in a heavy pan with a lid.

2. Add vegetables, sauté over medium heat while stirring together for 1-2 minutes.

3. Cover skillet and cook until vegetables begin to wilt, 6-8 minutes.

4. Remove lid, quickly drain accumulated water/juice.

5. Stir in rhubarb cooking sauce. Thoroughly heat.

Salt and pepper to taste.

Cranberry Hot Sauce

This can be kept in your refrigerator for several weeks in a closed glass container. When I was given this recipe, it called for cayenne powder, but I modified it because I like the bites of hot instead of all of it being hot.

One 16-oz. bag fresh cranberries (Remove bad ones.)

2 jalapeño peppers, seeded and chopped

½ cup sugar (Adjust according to taste.)

½ to 1 cup orange or cranberry juice, according to taste

1 tablespoon grated orange zest

Salt to taste

1. Put peppers, juices, and zest into a blender.

2. Blend at high speed until peppers are thoroughly chopped up.

3. Thoroughly mix together all ingredients.

4. Taste; add sugar if you prefer it sweeter.

5. Put in a heavy saucepan and boil over medium heat until berries pop, about 10 minutes.

6. Skim foam from surface with a slotted spoon.

7. Allow to cool before serving.

Whole Cranberry Salsa

This is my personal creation. Use as you would any salsa except for cheese dip; it turns the cheese purple. I particularly enjoy it on pork and poultry dark meat. Store in glass jars in your refrigerator. It will keep for several weeks and gets better with time.

---

1 cup red bell pepper, diced ¼-inch pieces
1 cup green bell pepper, diced ¼-inch pieces
1 cup yellow chili peppers, ¼-inch pieces
1 cup mild white onion, diced ¼-inch pieces
8 cups boiling water
One 16-oz. can whole berry cranberry sauce
2-4 tablespoons sugar (optional)
Salt to taste

1. Put peppers and onions in an oven-proof bowl and cover with boiling water.

2. Allow to cool to room temperature, about 2 hours.

3. Drain in colander for at least 10 minutes to get rid of water.

4. Mix salt and cranberry sauce into the chopped vegetables.

5. Taste. Add sugar if you prefer a sweeter salsa.

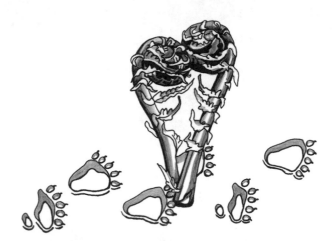

Zingy Fiddlehead Ferns

Fiddleheads are the unfolded leaves of ferns. They look like the top of a violin, hence the name. They are the first green edibles to sprout in the spring and are as welcome as is the first asparagus in the Lower 48.

---

1 lb. fresh fiddlehead ferns (Green beans, asparagus, celery strips may be substituted.)

4 cups water

½ cup vinegar

½ cup oil

¼ cup lemon juice

8 chunks crystallized ginger

1 teaspoon coriander seeds

1-2 jalapeño peppers cut in half

2 teaspoons salt

1. Combine water, vinegar, lemon juice, oil, and salt in a large enameled pot.

2. Mix coriander, ginger, and pepper in a tea ball or double-layered cheesecloth bag.

3. Put spice ball into pot with liquids.

4. Bring to a boil, then reduce heat to low.

5. Stir in fiddleheads.

6. Simmer until ferns are just tender. You want the ferns to be tender yet crunchy.

7. Remove and discard spices in tea ball.

8. Allow fiddleheads to cool, then refrigerate for at least 2 hours to thoroughly chill. Longer cooling times increase the flavor.

9. Serve as an appetizer either alone or with a favorite dipping sauce.

Kelp Bulb Pickles

Harvest your kelp at sea if you can; anything on the beach is usually sandy and may have been there for a while. If you use kelp from the beach, remember the more rubbery kelp are not as fresh, and rinse the heck out of them.

---

8 lbs. bulb kelp
2 cups salt
½ teaspoon alum
7 cups sugar
4 cups cider vinegar
½ teaspoon oil of cloves
½ teaspoon oil of cinnamon

1. Cut kelp into 12-inch lengths.

2. Using a vegetable peeler, remove dark surface layer.

3. Dissolve salt in two gallons of water.

4. Soak kelp in salt water for eight hours. Be sure and

keep kelp completely covered by brine.

5. Remove and drain.

6. Cut kelp into ½-inch pieces.

7. Dissolve alum in ½ gallon water.

8. Soak kelp in alum-water for 15 minutes.

9. Drain kelp in cold water.

10. Throw away water and rinse kelp again in more water.

11. Put kelp in enamel pan and cover with boiling water.

12. Cook until kelp can be pierced with a fork. Be careful not to overcook.

13. Drain and return kelp to enamel pan.

14. Combine sugar, vinegar, and oils.

15. Bring to a boil and cook for 2 minutes.

16. Pour sugar mixture over kelp.

17. Let stand for 8 hours.

18. Drain syrup and reheat.

19. Pour hot syrup over kelp and let stand for 24 hours.

20. Reheat kelp and syrup.

21. Place in glass jars and seal immediately.

Kohlrabi-Mushroom Soup

Kohlrabi is another underappreciated vegetable that loves Alaska, and I admit I never ate it until I arrived. Incidentally kohlrabi can run to 60 pounds in the Land of the Midnight Sun. Stick with the smaller ones. They taste a lot better.

---

1 onion, chopped
1 clove garlic, minced
½ lb. mushrooms, sliced
¼ cup oil
One 14½-oz. can tomatoes, coarsely chopped
4 cups stock, moose, beef, or chicken
4 kohlrabi, peeled and sliced into ¼-inch slices
1 tablespoon dill, fresh chopped
Salt and pepper to taste

1. In a medium saucepan, heat oil until smoky.

2. Sauté onion, garlic, and mushrooms over medium-high heat until the onions are limp.

3. Add the tomatoes and cook for another 3-5 minutes.

4. Add stock, bring to a boil.

5. Stir in the kohlrabi.

6. Lower the heat and simmer for 15 minutes or until kohlrabi is done.

7. Correct seasonings and top with dill.

Potato Croquettes

Think of it as your own, homemade tater tots.

---

2 cups cold mashed potatoes; salt and pepper to taste

1 tablespoon butter, melted

2 eggs, separated

Flour or cracker crumbs

Lard or shortening for frying

1. Mix mashed potatoes, salt, pepper and butter together.

2. Beat the whites of two eggs, and work into potatoes.

3. Make small balls.

4. Slightly flatten balls.

5. Dip them into beaten egg yolks and roll in flour or crumbs.

6. Fry in hot shortening.

7. Serve immediately.

Potato and Kielbasa Soup

This isn't your traditional potato soup.

¾ lb. kielbasa, sliced into thin coins
1 onion, chopped
2-3 tablespoons oil
2 lbs. potatoes, chopped into ½-inch chunks
1 bay leaf
6 cups stock, moose, beef, or chicken broth
One 10-oz. package of frozen peas, thawed
½ cup green onions, chopped

1. Sauté kielbasa and onions in oil until sausage is lightly browned in a large stockpot (at least 10 quarts) over medium-high heat.

2. Pour off fat and return pot to heat.

3. Add potatoes, bay leaf, and stock.

4. Bring to a boil, reduce heat to medium, and simmer until potatoes are cooked, 8-12 minutes.

5. Remove bay leaf and discard.

6. Transfer a cup or so of stock and potatoes to blender and puree until smooth.

7. Repeat until about half of the potatoes are pureed and stock is thick.

8. Add peas and simmer until heated through, 4-6 minutes.

9. Garnish with green onions, and serve.

Rhubarb Cooking Sauce

This is another one of my creations. Go easy on the peppers the first time you make this. This is a very fiery sauce. Warning: Wear gloves when handling the peppers. Rinse your gloves and your hands when done.

Step One:

> 4 cups rhubarb, cut into ¼- to ½-inch pieces
> ½ cup sugar
> ½ to 1 cup orange juice or water

1. Mix rhubarb and sugar.

2. Allow to sit for at least 15 minutes, 1-2 hours is better. This draws juice from rhubarb.

3. Pour rhubarb and juice into blender and blend until rhubarb is completely broken up into a pulp. If rhubarb is "dry" add orange juice or water. Start blending at slow speed and then gradually increase speed.

4. Pour into a medium saucepan and bring to a boil over medium high heat. Stir to prevent scorching.

5. When mixture reaches a boil, reduce to simmer and simmer uncovered until pulp thickens and rhubarb is done. Stir often. This takes 10-15 minutes.

6. Remove from heat and allow to cool. Sauce thickens as it cools.

Step Two:

> 2 cups rhubarb sauce from step one
> 1 cup corn oil
> 4-8 garlic cloves
> ½ cup chopped onion
> 1 juice of lemon

1 tablespoon Worcestershire sauce
1 to 3 habanero peppers
Salt to taste

1. Combine all ingredients in blender.

2. Blend until completely combined and smooth. It will be a deep pink.

Rhubarb Ketchup

Similar recipes substitute cranberries for the rhubarb.

4 cups rhubarb, diced
1 teaspoon cinnamon
1 teaspoon ground cloves
1 teaspoon allspice
2½ cups sugar
1 cup vinegar
1 tablespoon ground cayenne
Water, as needed

1. Slice the rhubarb along the rib. An average piece of rhubarb should be split into four or five strips.

2. Keep the rhubarb strips together and cut across the rib so that each piece is less than ¼ inch long.

3. Stir everything together.

4. Simmer for one hour. Stir regularly to prevent scorching. Add a little water if it gets too dry while cooking.

5. Store in sterilized glass jars.

Spinach Supreme

This makes an attractive dish when served in the peppers and tomatoes. It was the first vegetable recipe given to me after I arrived in Alaska.

---

1 lb. fresh spinach (or one 10-oz. package of frozen spinach)

2 cups sour cream

1 package dry onion soup mix

1 cup bread crumbs

4 medium tomatoes (optional)

4 medium bell peppers (optional)

1. Remove stems from spinach and carefully wash each leave to remove grit.

2. Slice spinach into thin strips. If using frozen spinach, defrost first.

3. Boil spinach in a small amount of salted water for 3-5 minutes.

4. Thoroughly drain spinach.

5. Squeeze spinach dry.

6. Mix together spinach, sour cream, and onion soup mix.

7. Cut tops off tomatoes and bell peppers.

8. Remove seeds and pulp from tomatoes and bell peppers.

9. Stuff tomatoes and bell peppers with spinach mixture. Top with bread crumbs.

10. Bake for 30 minutes at 325 degrees. If you do not stuff peppers and tomatoes, top mixture with bread crumbs, and bake in an oven proof pan.

Stir-Fried Spinach

Cook at the last minute and serve immediately. I take it to the table in the frying pan or cook it in a wok at the table. And I never salt it. I leave that up to my guests.

---

1 lb. fresh spinach
4 green onions, sliced into ¼-inch pieces
3-4 cloves garlic, minced
1 cup mushrooms, chopped or sliced thin
1 tablespoon sesame oil
1 tablespoon oil
Salt and pepper to taste

1. Thoroughly wash spinach, one leaf at a time.

2. Dry spinach.

3. Tear spinach into smaller pieces, removing and discarding stems.

4. Using medium high heat, stir-fry onions, mushrooms, and garlic in oils until limp, about two minutes.

5. Add spinach and stir-fry for 1-2 minutes or until spinach is slightly wilted.

6. Season and serve immediately.

Mashed Turnips and Potatoes with Garlic

This is a traditional dish that has gone out of favor. Turnips add a bit of bite to complement the blander potatoes.

1 lb. turnips, peeled, cut into ½-inch chunks
1 lb. potatoes, peeled, cut into ½-inch chunks
4 cloves garlic, peeled and minced
¼ cup butter
2 tablespoons sour cream
Milk at room temperature

1. In a large pot of salted boiling water cook turnips, potatoes, and garlic until tender, 10-12 minutes.

2. Drain and mash turnips, potatoes, and garlic.

3. Stir in butter and sour cream.

4. If too thick, stir in milk, 2-3 tablespoons at a time.

Salt and pepper to taste.

Turnip Soup

Similar to many potato soups. Don't skip the sauerkraut juice; it adds a special zing. For more variety, add cut up carrots, green peas, and other vegetables.

---

1 lb. beef stew meat cut into ½-inch cubes

1 lb. soup bones

¼ lb. ham meat, cut into chunks

1 lb. turnip, cubed

1 cup sauerkraut juice

2 onions, sliced

1 sprig parsley, chopped

6-10 peppercorns, whole

1 teaspoon marjoram

4 cloves garlic, minced

2 tablespoons fresh dill, chopped

Sour cream

1. Add beef, ham, soup bones, and peppercorns to large pot (at least 8 quarts) and top with boiling water.

2. Simmer for 1½ to 2 hours.

3. Remove bones and skim.

4. Extract meat from bones and return to soup. Dispose of bones.

5. Add turnips, onions, parsley, marjoram, and sauerkraut juice.

6. Simmer, partially covered, until turnips are soft, 45-60 minutes.

7. Serve with sour cream and fresh dill.

Salt and pepper to taste.

Stuffed Zucchini

How else will you get rid of the zucchini that your neighbors and co-workers insist on giving you? You can only eat so much zucchini bread.

---

4 zucchini, ½ lb. each, split in half
½ lb. mushrooms, finely chopped
¼ tablespoon butter
1 cup onion, finely chopped
1 tablespoon garlic, finely minced
2 teaspoons lemon juice
¼ teaspoon thyme
1 cup bread crumbs
¼ cup parsley, finely chopped
¼ cup parmesan, grated
1 egg yolk
2 tablespoons oil
Salt and pepper to taste

1. Preheat oven to 450 degrees.

2. Scoop out center of the zucchini, leaving a shell at least ¼ inch thick.

3. Save pulp and finely chop.

4. Add enough water to cover the shells into a saucepan and bring to a boil.

5. Add the shells and simmer 2 minutes.

6. Drain thoroughly.

7. Heat butter in heavy skillet and sauté mushrooms, onions, and garlic until limp, 3-5 minutes.

8. Add lemon juice, chopped zucchini, thyme, salt, and pepper. Cook about three minutes until the excess moisture evaporates. Stir to avoid sticking.

9. Remove from heat and cool.

10. When cooled, mix with most of the bread crumbs (save a little for topping), parsley, half the cheese, and blend thoroughly.

11. Stir in the egg yolk.

12. Spoon an equal portion of the filling into each zucchini shell.

13. Mix the remaining bread crumbs and cheese and sprinkle over the top of the stuffed zucchini.

14. Sprinkle stuffed zucchinis evenly with the two tablespoons oil.

15. Apply cooking spray to the inside of a baking dish big enough to hold the shells in one layer.

16. Add stuffed zucchini and bake 25 minutes.

17. Serve immediately.

Meat

Long before the first words were ever written, Alaska's earliest residents ate meat. In all likelihood, the first recipe used in Alaska—and passed down through the generations—was:

1. Catch animal.

2. Eat animal.

Of course recipes change and evolve with new advances in kitchen appliances, tastes, and sophistication. Recipes reflect these changes, and the basic meat recipe probably evolved into:

1. Catch animal.

2. Kill animal.

3. Eat animal.

Generations between those and ours added such refinements as cooking the animal, removing skin, fur, and feathers.

Alaska never has been the best place for vegetarians. Northern cuisine relies heavily on red meat. Bacon in particular has a special place in Alaska's eating habits.

The first soldiers, explorers, and miners depended on bacon and other cured meats for months at a time. Fresh meat supplemented and, when hunting was good, replaced the imported meat. But cured meats were about the only options that could be stored.

Cured ham was more than a basic ration for hungry humans. According to Dermot Cole's *Fairbanks: A Gold Rush Town That Beat the Odds*, electrical power plant operators threw hundreds of pounds of bacon into the boiler during Fairbanks' great fire of 1906. The fatty bacon ignited, creating a hotter fire and generating more steam and power for the water pumps. With the extra water, fire fighters extinguished the fire, but only after much of the business district went up in smoke. Residents reported Fairbanks smelling like burnt pork for days. By some accounts bears from the surrounding hills followed their noses into town looking for a treat.

Habits change slowly, and today Spam and canned hams readily sell. Only Hawaiians eat more Spam than residents of the North. With today's air freight, almost any food is available fresh, but Alaskans still enjoy their cured meats. It's part of their tradition—even when they stir-fry it with teriyaki sauce.

Three quick reminders on cooking game meat: Since it is lower in fat than domestic meats, it cooks faster and also dries out faster. Meat flavors come from their fats. Careful trimming of visible fat reduces the game flavor for people who dislike it. Domestically raised game meats (those purchased at a specialty meat store) generally have been fed a diet similar to domestic beef, poultry, and pork. Domestic raised game meats tend to be milder and fatter than wild game meat harvested by a hunter.

Hunter's Pie

You could call this a Game Meat Shepherd's Pie. The parmesan cheese is a modern, post-pipeline addition to a traditional recipe.

---

3 tablespoons oil

1 turnip, peeled and cut into ½-inch chunks

2 stalks celery, cut into ½-inch chunks

1 onion, peeled and cut into ½-inch chunks

3-4 carrots, peeled and cut into ½-inch coins

3 cloves garlic, peeled and minced

1-2 lbs. game meat (venison, caribou, moose, bear, sheep), fat removed, cut into ½-inch chunks

2-3 tablespoons flour

1-2 cups meat stock or water

1 tablespoon tomato paste

Salt to taste

½ teaspoon cayenne pepper

½ teaspoon black pepper

Potato Topping:

3 lbs. potatoes, peeled and cut into large pieces

½ cup milk, room temperature

2 tablespoons butter, room temperature

3-4 tablespoons parmesan cheese, grated (optional)

1. Preheat oven to 350 degrees.

2. Cover potatoes with cold water in a large pot and boil until fork tender.

3. Drain and mash until potatoes are free of lumps.

4. Add the butter and milk.

5. Mix and continue mashing.

6. Salt and pepper to taste.

7. Cover and set aside.

8. Heat oil in a large non-stick skillet over medium high heat.

9. Add vegetables and garlic.

10. Cook vegetables until softened, 8-10 minutes.

11. Sprinkle vegetables with flour.

12. Cook for another minute or two, stirring evenly to coat vegetables with flour.

13. Add stock and tomato paste.

14. Stir to blend until the vegetables are tender and liquid has mostly evaporated, about 5 five minutes. Mixture should be slightly thickened. Set aside.

15. In a non-stick skillet over medium heat, cook the meat.

16. Season with salt, cayenne and black pepper.

17. Cook the meat until it is completely done.

18. Drain the cooked meat.

19. Combine meat with vegetables.

20. Spread meat-vegetable mixture in the bottom of a large oven-proof casserole.

21. Top with mashed potatoes.

22. Sprinkle with cheese.

23. Brown in oven for approximately 15-20 minutes.

Sauerkraut and Pork

This should be served out of doors or in a well-ventilated space with understanding friends.

3 lbs. sauerkraut

1 lb. smoked pork chops or ham

3-4 apples, cored and chopped

1 lb. smoked sausage

Two 12-oz. cans beer*

1-2 lbs. potatoes, cut into 1-inch chunks

The first time you make this use a pilsner beer. But don't use light beer.

1. In a large Dutch oven, place a layer of kraut.

2. Top with half the smoked meat, apples, and sausage.

3. Add another layer of kraut.

4. Top with remaining meat.

5. Top with kraut.

6. Top with potatoes.

7. Add enough beer or water to cover (If you have beer left over, drink it.)

8. Bring to a boil, cover, and reduce to simmer.

9. Cook for 2 hours, adding more beer or water if it gets too dry.

10. Serve with more beer, dark bread and butter.

Roasted Beaver Tail

Accept no substitutes. Use only genuine North American beaver tail. Naturally Alaska beavers are best.

---

1 beaver tail
6-8 bacon slices
2 onions, sliced
4 tablespoons salt
½ cup vinegar
2 tablespoons baking soda
4 cups water

1. Mix a light brine.

2. Thoroughly wash beaver with the brine.

3. Mix four quarts water, the vinegar, and two tablespoons salt.

4. Soak beaver tail overnight in water, vinegar brine.

5. The next morning, drain the beaver tail, wash, and cover with 2 quarts fresh water, plus the soda.

6. Bring to a boil, reduce heat, and simmer for 10 minutes.

7. Drain, pat dry, and place beaver in roasting pan.

8. Salt and pepper the tail.

9. Cover with sliced onions and bacon.

10. Cover pan and bake at 375 degrees until tender.

Wild Duck

When you pluck the ducks, dig out the shot if you can. If not, at least mark where the shot went in and warn anyone eating the bird so they can cut their meat into small pieces. One power chomp on a cluster of birdshot could mean a trip to the dentist.

---

2 ducks
1 tablespoon salt
1 tablespoon pepper
1 apple, in large chunks
4 slices of thick-cut smoky bacon
1 onion, peeled and chopped

1. Wash and dry ducks.

2. Sprinkle each duck cavity with ½ teaspoon salt.

3. Mix together remaining salt and pepper.

4. Sprinkle over outside of duck.

5. Mix apple and onion.

6. Stuff body cavity with apple-onion mixture.

7. Lay two slices of bacon across breast of each duck.

8. Bake in 500-degree oven for 25-30 minutes.

Cranberry Moose Chili

Think of this as a northern sweet-and-sour chili. This makes a thick, meaty chili. If you prefer more liquid, add another can of beer or a cup or two of water. The cook may also require more beer.

---

2 lbs. coarse ground moose meat or beef
2 cups chopped onions
6 cloves of garlic, minced
½ lb. thick slices of smoky bacon, chopped
2-4 jalapeño peppers, seeded and chopped
One 16-oz. can cranberry sauce
4 tablespoons chili powder
Two 12-oz. cans beer for the recipe
Unknown number of 12-oz. cans beer for the cook
1 tablespoon beef soup granules
Salt and pepper to taste

1. In a large Dutch oven with a tight fitting lid, sauté bacon over low heat until limp (do not cook until crisp).

2. Add garlic, onions, peppers, and moose.

3. Increase heat to medium and cook until vegetables are limp and meat is browned.

4. Add beer, cranberry sauce, seasonings, and soup granules.

5. Cover and cook over medium low heat for 30-45 minutes. Stir periodically. Add liquid and reduce heat if chili becomes too thick.

Moose Chili #2

This is more of a traditional chili. Watch this after you add the corn meal. It can get too thick and scorch.

---

4 lbs. moose meat, coarsely ground

2-4 cups water

¼ to ½ cup corn meal

3 tablespoons oil

1 large onion, chopped

¼ to ½ cup chili powder

2 tablespoons garlic powder

Salt and pepper to taste

1. Sauté onion and meat in oil until meat is brown and onion is limp, 5-10 minutes.

2. Add water and cook over medium heat for 60-90 minutes; add water if chili becomes dry.

3. When meat is tender, check water and add more if necessary.

4. Bring to a boil.

5. Reduce to very low and stir in chili powder and garlic powder.

6. Simmer 15-20 minutes.

7. Stir in corn meal gradually to thicken. Add ¼ cup at first. The more corn meal you add, the thicker the chili will be.

8. Simmer another 10-15 minutes and serve.

Moose Barley Soup or Stew

Call it soup if watery; stew if thick. Serve it in a bowl and keep them guessing.

2-3 tablespoons oil

1 onion, chopped

1-2 teaspoons garlic powder

1-2 stalks celery, chopped

1 lb. beef or game meat, cut into ¼-inch pieces

2-3 carrots, peeled and cut into coins

½ cup pearl barley

5-8 cups meat stock (8 cups for soup; 5 for stew)

1 lb. mushrooms, cut up

1-3 tablespoons ground black pepper

Salt to taste

1. Brown onion, celery, garlic, moose, and mushrooms in oil using medium heat in a large pot.

2. Add stock and carrots, simmer partially covered until carrots are semi-soft, about 30 minutes.

3. Check frequently, add water if needed.

4. Skim top if foam forms.

5. Add barley and pepper, continue to simmer until carrots and barley are both soft, about 30 minutes.

6. When done, adjust seasoning, and serve.

Ptarmigan with Cabbage

If you can't find ptarmigan in your local supermarket, chicken thighs are an acceptable substitute. Substitute two or three chicken thighs for one ptarmigan.

3-4 ptarmigan
1 medium cabbage, shredded
¼ cup butter, lard, cooking oil, or bacon fat
¼ to ½ teaspoon red pepper, such as cayenne
Juniper berries
1 cup condensed milk or heavy cream

1. Parboil the shredded cabbage in salted water for 10 minutes.

2. Drain.

3. In a heavy pan, melt the fat and brown the ptarmigan over medium heat.

4. Add the cabbage, red pepper, and a few juniper berries.

5. Cover and cook for 20 minutes.

6. Add cream, mix well, and adjust the seasoning.

7. Cover and cook for another 10 minutes.

Rhubarbed Ptarmigan

This is even better as leftovers. They make great sandwiches if you remember to remove the bones. I prefer a crusty sourdough.

---

12 ptarmigan breasts (or 12 chicken, or
    4 turkey thighs)
2 cups rhubarb cooking sauce (See page 56.)
Salt and pepper to taste

1. Place three ptarmigan breasts (or three chicken thighs or one turkey thigh) in the middle of a sheet of aluminum foil.

2. Repeat to make a total of four packets.

3. Cover ptarmigan with ½ cup rhubarb cooking sauce.

4. Fold aluminum foil around ptarmigan to make a cooking packet.

5. Add another layer of foil to double wrap.

6. Place in campfire coals and bake for 30-50 minutes or until done. In an oven, bake at 325 degrees for 35-45 minutes.

Rabbit

Cheer up. You don't have to catch your own rabbit. The domesticated rabbits from rabbit farms that you find in the frozen section of your supermarket work beautifully. In fact, they are usually meatier and more tender than wild rabbits.

---

  1 rabbit, cut up
  ½ cup flour
  1 tablespoon salt
  ½ tablespoon pepper
  ¼ cup bacon grease (or oil)
  3 cups water
  2 onions, chopped
  3-6 bay leaves
  2 teaspoons curry powder (optional)

1. Wash and dry rabbit.

2. Mix salt, pepper, and flour.

3. Dredge rabbit in flour, salt, and pepper.

4. Heat grease to smoking over medium to medium-high heat.

5. Brown rabbit.

6. When rabbit is browned, remove.

7. Sauté onions in oil.

8. Add water, bay leaves, flour-pepper-salt mixture, and curry powder. Whisk the flour into liquid, crushing all lumps.

9. Add rabbit, cover, and simmer 1-2 hours.

10. Serve when rabbit is tender and gravy is thick.

Fried Rabbit

For many, this was the Sunday fried "chicken" dinner. Only, when times were lean and rabbits plentiful, it was every night.

---

1 rabbit, cut up
½ cup flour
1 tablespoon salt
½ teaspoon pepper
½ cup oil or bacon grease
½ cup hot water

1. Wash and dry cleaned rabbits.

2. Combine salt, pepper, and flour.

3. Dredge rabbit pieces in flour.

4. Heat oil until smoky over medium-high heat.

5. Brown floured rabbit on both sides.

6. Sprinkle rabbit with water.

7. Cover, reduce heat, and simmer until done, about 45 minutes.

8. Make gravy using flour, pan drippings, and additional water.

Reindeer

Caribou and reindeer are first cousins and taste about the same.

---

2 reindeer steaks, ¾-inch thick
½ cup oil, butter or bacon grease
3-4 onions, peeled and sliced into ½-inch slices
1-2 cloves garlic, minced

1. Heat a large, heavy frying pan to medium and add one-half the oil.

2. When smoky, add garlic and onions. Stir frequently.

3. Cook until brown, 8-10 minutes.

4. Remove to a warm plate.

5. Melt remaining butter and, when smoky, add steaks.

6. Gently fry for about 5 minutes on each side. Do not overcook. The steaks should be pink inside.

7. When steaks are done, serve smothered by onions.

Cranberry Venison Meatballs

This is a northern twist on an old favorite.

2 cups bread crumbs

One 16-oz. can cranberry sauce

½ cup milk

One 8-oz. can tomato sauce

3 eggs

3 lbs. ground venison

½ cup onions, finely chopped

Oil

Salt, pepper

Flour

Water

1. Combine crumbs, cranberry sauce, milk, tomato sauce, and eggs in a large mixing bowl.

2. Let stand for a few minutes.

3. Add meat, onions, salt, and pepper.

4. Form meatballs 1 to 1½ inches in diameter.

5. Roll meatballs in flour.

6. Brown meatballs, a few at a time, in a little oil in a large heavy frying pan at medium heat.

7. When meatballs are browned, put them in a single layer in an oven-proof baking dish.

8. Add ¼ inch of water to dish. Cover meatballs with foil.

9. Bake for 30 minutes at 350 degrees.

10. Remove foil, turn meatballs, add ¼ inch of water.

11. Bake another 10-15 minutes until brown.

Venison Roast

This recipe is deliberately vague. Cooking times will depend on the size of the roast. Do not cook until well done, or it will be dry and stringy. Medium well or slightly pink should be the goal.

---

1 venison leg roast, fat removed
½ to 1 lb. smoky bacon, thick slice
Bacon drippings or shortening
Salt, pepper
2-6 onions, peeled and halved or quartered
2-6 potatoes or turnips, cut into 2-inch pieces
2-6 carrots, peeled and cut into 2-inch pieces
Water

1. Salt and pepper roast.

2. In a large roasting pan with high sides sear the meat in the bacon drippings.

3. Lay slices of bacon over roast.

4. Put vegetables around roast in pan.

5. Bake at 350 degrees for 2-4 hours.

6. Check frequently and, if no liquid forms in the pan, add a cup of water.

7. Add water as needed, but be careful not to add too much.

8. Baste with pan drippings every 20 minutes or so.

9. When cooked, remove from oven and let rest for about 20 minutes before cutting.

Venison Roast with Beer

Venison, like all game meat, should have all fat removed. The gamey flavor that many people object to comes from the fat.

One 3- to 4-lb. venison roast
Two 12-oz. cans beer. Dark beers are best.
Garlic pepper
Oil
2-4 tablespoons flour
Water

1. Season roast with pepper.

2. Brown roast in oil over medium heat.

3. Place browned roast in oven-proof pan with sides.

4. Add ½ can of beer.

5. Bake for 1½ to 2½ hours in a 325-degree oven.

6. Check every 30 minutes while cooking and add ½ can of beer when needed.

7. Check for tenderness and, when done, remove from oven.

8. While meat rests, combine pan drippings with flour and water or beer for gravy.

Fish

Who can think of Alaska and not think of salmon?

Five different species of Pacific salmon return each year to spawn and start another generation. Some swim the length of the Yukon River into Canada, the equivalent of swimming from Chicago to LA. For uncounted generations, local peoples have harvested the fish. They kept the best species for themselves and fed chum salmon to their dogs—hence, the local name of dog salmon.

When salmon enter fresh water on the way to their ancestral spawning ground, they quit eating and subsist entirely off fat reserves. This substantially changes the flavor. You can usually tell where an Alaskan calls home by his or her salmon preference. Coastal Alaskans want only fish caught in salt water, while Interior residents often find salt water fish "bland" compared to the river fish they grew up eating.

Yet, salmon are only one of the many wonderful fish that flourish in Alaska's waters. Coastal residents feast on halibut, lingcod, sea bass, shark, eel, herring, and other varieties. They also get to enjoy prawns, three species of crabs, and shellfish. A warning: Eat shellfish only from an approved beach. Paralytic Shellfish Poison contaminates many Alaskan beaches. Burbot—also called lingcod, but a different species from the popular salt water fish of the same name—join trout, grayling, and other freshwater fish on Interior menus.

Surimi is a manufactured fish product camouflaged to pass off as crab and prawns. It is made from flakes of real fish—frequently hake—glued together with egg whites and artificial flavoring and coloring. It is commonly found on low-budget, all-you-can-eat buffet lines.

Seafood Casserole

Zucchini and salmon arrive in great numbers about the same time every year. Grilled together with a bit of dill they make a good meal. Add the following and they make a great meal.

---

4 potatoes
2-3 cups water
1 cup evaporated milk (You may substitute fresh milk.)
2 tablespoons butter
2 chicken bullion cubes
1 teaspoon onion powder
2 cloves garlic, minced
1 large onion, chopped
1 bell pepper, cut into strips

One 14½-oz. can stewed tomatoes, drained
(Save the liquid.)

1 bay leaf

1 teaspoon basil leaves

¼ teaspoon thyme

1 cup mushrooms

2 small zucchini, cut into 1-inch chunks

2 tablespoons parsley

1 lb. salmon, cooked or raw (You may substitute
shrimp or crab meat.)

¼ teaspoon pepper

1. Combine one potato, bullion cubes, onion powder, and 1 cup water.

2. Bring to a boil, cover, and simmer until potato is tender, about 10 minutes.

3. When done, blend potato and water until smooth.

4. Stir in milk.

5. Blend until smooth, add more milk if needed.

6. Set aside.

7. Cut 2 potatoes in ¾-inch chunks.

8. Combine potatoes, garlic, onion, bell pepper, stewed tomatoes, bay leaf, basil, thyme, and 1 cup water.

9. Bring to a boil, reduce heat, and simmer with cover on, 10 minutes.

10. Add mushrooms, zucchini and parsley.

11. Simmer 5 minutes.

12. Discard bay leaf.

13. Preheat oven to 350 degrees.

14. Pour mixture into a shallow casserole dish.

15. Stir in salmon and cover with the blended potato milk sauce.

16. Slice last potato ¼-inch thick and top mixture and then cover with foil.

17. Bake 20 minutes or until fish is tender and sauce is bubbly.

Alaskan Seafood Stir-Fry

Using a mixture of red, green, and yellow peppers adds color to the dish.

2-3 tablespoons oil
1-3 jalapeño peppers, sliced into thin slivers
8-12 garlic cloves, peeled, coarsely chopped
6-8 green onions, sliced into ½-inch pieces
1 medium bell pepper, sliced into thin strips
1 lb. mushrooms, sliced into thick chunks
1 lb. shrimp or scallops

1. Heat oil to 375 degrees in a wok.

2. Add hot peppers, onion, and garlic and sauté 2-3 minutes. This merges the flavors of the garlic and pepper with the oil.

3. Add mushrooms and bell pepper and sauté 2-5 minutes depending on how "done" you want your mushrooms.

4. Add seafood and sauté until done, about 2-5 minutes.

5. Serve over rice or pasta.

Alaska Seafood Chowder

Traditionally, this is served with pilot bread, but saltine crackers can be substituted.

---

6 cups fish, any firm meat fish
1 cup crab meat
1 cup shrimp meat
6 strips bacon
2 onions, chopped
2 stalks celery, chopped
4-5 potatoes, peeled, cut into ½-inch chunks
2-4 cups fish stock, chicken stock, or water
2 cans evaporated milk (Fresh milk is OK.)
¼ cup flour
Salt, pepper to taste

1. Dice the bacon and sauté with onion and celery in large pot until limp.

2. Add cubed fish, potatoes, and enough water to cover.

3. Cook over medium heat until potatoes are tender.

4. Add crab and shrimp and simmer for 4-8 minutes. Do not overcook!

5. Thoroughly stir flour into evaporated milk.

6. Reduce heat and slowly stir milk-flour into pot. Do not boil!

7. When chowder thickens, salt and pepper to taste.

8. Serve.

Fish Chowder

This is Alaska's answer to the clam chowder of the east coast. Peppered bacon is a relatively new item in the north, but a readily accepted addition.

2 lbs. mild white fish (cod, halibut, burbot, ling cod, etc.), chopped into 1-inch pieces

¼ lb. thick-sliced bacon (or peppered bacon), chopped

2 onions, chopped

One 16-oz. can corn

2 lbs. potatoes, chopped into small chunks

3 cans evaporated milk

Water

Salt, pepper to taste

1. Sauté bacon and onions over low heat until bacon and onions are limp and fat is released.

2. Add milk, fish, potatoes, corn. Cook over medium to medium-low heat until fish and potatoes are done, about 20-25 minutes. Milk should barely cover all ingredients. If not, add more milk or a little water. Stir several times during cooking and add more milk or water if it needs more liquid.

3. Five minutes or so before serving add pepper.

4. Serve with crackers.

Seafood Brine for Smoked Salmon

Many Alaskans have their own secret recipe for brine. Alaskan smoking brines are as personal as Tennessee or Texas barbeque sauce.

Consider this as a starter brine that will change as your personal smoking style develops. And, for the record, this is not my secret family brine. Some things just aren't for sharing.

---

2 cups salt
2 cups brown sugar
10-16 cups water

1. Mix salt and brown sugar together. Break up lumps.

2. Stir salt and sugar into ten cups of water.

3. Taste. If the brine is too salty, dilute with additional water.

4. Soak overnight fish cut into ½- to 1-inch thick slices.

5. Put fish on smoking racks and allow to drip for at least one hour to get rid of excess brine.

6. Smoke.

Smoked Salmon Potato Salad

Here's a mouth-watering northern summer salad with all fresh ingredients.

---

2 lbs. potatoes
½ cup vinegar and oil salad dressing
¼ cup dill, preferably fresh-chopped
2-3 cups broccoli, lightly cooked and chopped
¼ lb. smoked salmon, cut into thin strips
2-3 heads bibb lettuce, washed and trimmed

1. Cut potatoes into ¼-inch slices.

2. Boil potatoes until tender, but firm.

3. Drain potatoes and refrigerate to cool.

4. Combine dressing, dill, and chopped broccoli.

5. Stir in potatoes and smoked salmon.

6. Serve on lettuce leaves.

Potato Salmon Bisque

Salmon can be cooked or raw. This is a great use for leftover poached salmon.

---

1 cup salmon, bones and skin removed

2 cups chicken broth

2 tablespoons butter or oil

1½ cups milk or cream

4 green onions, chopped

1 tablespoon lemon juice

¼ to ½ teaspoon pepper

1 cup mashed potatoes (You may substitute ½ cup instant mashed potatoes.)

1. Sauté green onions in butter over medium heat until limp.

2. Add chicken broth and milk.

3. When warm, stir in mashed potatoes to make a thick soup.

4. Add salmon, lemon juice, and pepper.

5. Simmer over medium low heat until thoroughly heated.

6. Serve immediately.

Pickled Salmon

Use the freshest salmon possible. I like my fish firm, and fresh salmon is firmer. Fish is more completely pickled after four or five days.

---

1 cup water

1 cup white vinegar

¼ cup sugar

1 teaspoon salt

1 onion, sliced thin

1-2 lemons, sliced thin

1 tablespoon mustard seeds

1 teaspoon peppercorns

2-4 bay leaves

1 cup dill, preferably fresh

2 lbs. salmon skinned, cut into small pieces

1. Combine all ingredients except dill and salmon.

2. Bring to a boil over medium-high heat. Stir to mix.

3. When sugar melts, remove from heat and cool.

4. Put fish and dill in a glass container.

5. Pour the cooled liquid solution over fish. Make sure fish is completely covered.

6. Cover and refrigerate for at least 24 hours.

Salmon Loaf

There are a lot more salmon than beef cattle in Alaska.

---

2 cups cooked salmon, flaked, skin and bones
removed

2-3 pieces white bread, torn into small pieces

½ cup onion, minced

¼ cup milk

2 eggs

2 tablespoons parsley, chopped

1 tablespoon lemon juice

½ teaspoon dill weed, chopped

Salt and pepper to taste

1. Drain and flake salmon.

2. Thoroughly mix all ingredients together.

3. Grease an 8½- by 4½- by 2½-inch loaf pan.

4. Bake at 350 degrees for 45 minutes.

Salmon Patties

Until he tried patties with fresh salmon, my father refused to eat salmon. During the Depression, he had eaten canned salmon for days on end because it was cheap and he was broke. He liked these so much he had seconds.

2 cups salmon, boned

2 eggs

1 cup bread crumbs

½ cup milk

1 teaspoon lemon juice

Salt and pepper to taste

Cracker crumbs

Oil for cooking

1. Combine salmon, one egg, bread crumbs, milk, and lemon juice.

2. Thoroughly mix.

3. Refrigerator for at least 15 minutes.

4. Remove from refrigerator and make patties.

5. Beat second egg.

6. Dip patties into egg.

7. Dredge in cracker crumbs.

8. Fry in hot oil until brown.

Poached Salmon

The leftovers are even better than the first night. I frequently cook a day in advance and refrigerate. And like so many other recipes, this is just one of many versions.

---

4 salmon steaks, 8 oz. each

1 cup dry white wine

3 cups water

Dill, generous handful

¼ cup whole peppercorns

Salt and pepper to taste

1. Layer salmon steaks, over dill, in a single layer in a shallow skillet. Do not crowd.

2. Lightly salt and pepper.

3. Completely cover salmon with water and wine.

4. Add peppercorns.

5. Slowly bring to a gentle simmer.

6. Reduce heat to low, cover, and simmer until salmon is opaque, approximately 5-10 minutes.*

7. Turn heat off and let stand covered on burner for at least 10 minutes

8. Remove salmon steaks from poaching liquid.

9. Blot both sides of fish with paper towels, and serve.

This is approximate. You will need to cook it a few times to get the timing just right. Fortunately, since it is poached, you won't dry out the fish if you cook it too long the first time you try.

Salmon Dip

This is a common treat at Alaska wine-and-cheese gatherings as well as holidays. It's as much a fixture as the turkey at Thanksgiving. And, yes, everyone has a secret recipe.

½ lb. smoked salmon, flaked and skin removed

Two 8-oz. packages cream cheese

½ cup onions, finely chopped

½ cup mayonnaise

½ tablespoon garlic powder

1 tablespoon lemon juice

2-3 tablespoons creamed horseradish

1. Combine all ingredients.

2. Thoroughly blend.

3. Serve with crackers.

Stink Heads

Stink heads are judged by the number of days they are buried. Three-day, six-day, and nine-day are the "ages" I've most commonly heard. Nor have I personally tasted any older than nine days

---

Several salmon heads, any variety

Enough skunk cabbage leaves, cleaned

One shovel (or, more than one, if you have assistants)

1. Carefully wrap one salmon head in one or more skunk cabbage leaves.

2. Repeat until all heads are wrapped.

3. Bury in the ground, deep enough so that wolves, dogs, and foxes won't dig up.

4. Forget until ready to dig up.

5. Dig up.

6. Unwrap the skunk cabbage leaves and discard.

7. Eat the stink heads.

Disclaimer: Please do not roll bluegill heads in lawn clippings and think you are making genuine stink heads. Substitutions will not work. Soil temperatures are critical. You need the near frozen Alaskan summer soil to make real stink heads properly. Lower 48 soil is just too warm. Try that, and instead of genuine stink heads, you will have compost, but that is good for your garden.

Russian Salmon Pie

Feel free to add extra ingredients, peas, chopped celery, etc. Although not traditional, I serve my Russian salmon pie with soy sauce.

---

 4 cups cooked rice
 1-2 cups cooked salmon
 2 onions, chopped
 2-4 hard cooked eggs, shelled and sliced
 Salt and pepper to taste
 Pie crust

1. Preheat oven to 325 degrees.

2. Layer either a deep pie dish or cake pan with crust.

3. Mix rice, onions, and salmon together.

4. Lightly pack rice, onion, and salmon into pie crust.

5. Top with hard-cooked eggs.

6. Salt and pepper.

7. Cover with sheet of pie crust.

8. Cut three or four slits into the crust;

9. Bake for approximately 1 hour.

10. Cool for 10-20 minutes before serving.

Manifold Roasted Salmon

(Or how to cook a salmon on the boat's inboard or inboard/outboard engine while returning from a fishing trip).

Always use LOTS of foil. Too little and no matter what seasoning you use, the fish will taste like 10-30 or 10-40 motor oil depending on which you use in your engine. Also, ALWAYS make sure you firmly secure the salmon onto the manifold or it will slip and your entire boat will smell like salmon burnt in engine oil. Not that I ever had that experience of course. And besides it wasn't my boat.

One king salmon (at least 12 pounds cleaned)
Seasonings*
Aluminum foil (lots)
Bailing wire

Because this is a "boat recipe," use whatever you have on the boat, which may be as little as salt and pepper.

1. Clean the salmon leaving the head on.

2. Season.

3. Wrap in no fewer than five layers of foil, completely sealing the salmon.

4. Using bailing wire, firmly secure the foil-wrapped salmon onto the engine's manifold. Be careful not to break the foil.

5. Drive home. Cooking time will vary, but a 12-pound salmon takes 2-4 hours. Different engines run at different temperatures.

Salmon Potato Pancakes

It is critical to squeeze out as much liquid as possible from potatoes.

---

2 cups potatoes, peeled and coarsely grated*

½ cup smoked salmon, flaked, skin and bones removed

3 or 4 eggs

2 tablespoons flour

2 green onions, chopped

1-2 teaspoons salt

Oil for cooking

For a different taste, substitute grated zucchini, carrots, or turnips for ½ cup of potatoes. But it is still important to remove as much moisture as possible.

1. Squeeze as much liquid as possible from the potatoes.

2. Whisk the eggs until well blended.

3. Add potatoes, salmon, flour, onions, and salt.

4. Thoroughly mix.

5. Heat oil over medium to medium-high heat.

6. Drop spoonfuls of pancake mixture into pan and flatten. Pancakes should be about ¼-inch thick.

7. Cook until crisp, about three-to-five minutes on each side, and serve.

Creamed Halibut

Here's a different way to use leftover halibut.

1 cup halibut, cooked and flaked
4 tablespoons butter
3 tablespoons flour
2 cups milk, hot
Dash of cayenne
1 tablespoon lemon juice
1 green onion, minced
½ cup green peas, cooked
2 eggs, hard-boiled and chopped
½ cup dry bread crumbs
Salt and pepper to taste

1. Melt two tablespoons butter over medium heat.

2. Stir in flour and cook about 1 minute until thick.

3. Add hot milk, stirring constantly until sauce thickens.

4. Remove from heat.

5. Stir in cayenne and lemon juice.

6. Add halibut, green onion, peas, and chopped eggs.

7. Pour into a small buttered casserole and top with the remaining butter mixed with crumbs.

8. Bake at 350 degrees until the crumbs brown, about 15-20 minutes.

Halibut Pot Roast

Here's a fish lover's answer to the Yankee pot roast.

3-4 lb. boneless halibut roast, skin removed
1 cup flour
½ cup oil
5-6 carrots, peeled and cut into 1-inch lengths
5-6 onions, peeled and quartered
4-6 celery ribs, cut into 1-inch lengths
6-8 potatoes, quartered
2 cloves garlic, minced
2-3 cups water
Salt and pepper to taste

1. Roll halibut in flour.

2. Using medium to medium-high heat, heat oil.

3. Brown halibut in oil on all sides in large Dutch oven with tight fitting lid.

4. Arrange vegetables around halibut.

5. Add water, cover and bake at 350 degrees until halibut flakes and vegetables are done.

6. Remove roast and vegetables.

7. Thicken pan liquid and serve over halibut.

Halibut Supreme

This is a popular Alaskan dish that has many different names. Make extra when you prepare this. It's better the second day. But you have to make a lot because your guests will devour it. I have had friends surrounding the pan and scrapping the bottom with bread after they consumed every bit of the fish. I am serious; people like this.

In 1976, I helped cook more than 300 pounds of Halibut Supreme for a political rally. Not one of the more than 200 people attending complained. And there were no leftovers for the cooks to take home either.

---

2 lbs. halibut, bones and skin removed
2 cups dry white wine
1 cup white onion, finely chopped
2 cups sour cream*
1 cup mayonnaise*
1 cup dry white bread crumbs, sourdough
1 tablespoon paprika (optional)
Use the real stuff; low fat doesn't work.

1. Slice halibut into the size of fish sticks.

2. Marinate the halibut in the wine for at least 2 hours, but in no case longer than 24 hours, in your refrigerator.

3. Drain fish and pat dry.

4. Roll in bread crumbs.

5. Apply cooking spray to an oven-proof pan.

6. Place fish one layer thick with space between them in the pan.

7. Mix together the sour cream, mayonnaise, and chopped onion.

8. Cover fish with the mixture. Be sure to fill in the spaces between the pieces of fish.

9. Sprinkle with leftover bread crumbs and paprika.

10. Bake for 20-25 minutes at 450 degrees. When done, it will be bubbly and have a coarse custard consistency.

Garlic-Lemon Alaskan Halibut

Substitute other flavors such as ginger for a different taste sensation. Halibut is versatile. Use it with lemon and another lemon compatible flavor and you'll probably enjoy it.

---

4 halibut steaks, 1 to 1½ inches thick
4 tablespoons butter
1 tablespoon garlic, minced
1 tablespoon lemon pepper
Lemon juice

1. Season halibut steaks on both sides with lemon pepper.

2. Melt butter in large skillet over medium-high heat.

3. Stir in garlic.

4. Cook steaks in pan for 5-8 minutes per side. When fully cooked, the fish will flake when tested with a fork.

5. Season with lemon juice before serving.

Halibut Poached With Shrimp

This is an incredibly tasty dish for company.

½ cup sour cream
½ cup Alaska pink shrimp, meat only
1 tablespoon mayonnaise
¼ teaspoon dill weed
2 halibut steaks, 1-inch thick
1 onion, sliced
1 lemon, sliced
6-12 peppercorns

1. Combine sour cream, shrimp, dill and mayonnaise.

2. Cover and refrigerate at least 1 hour.

3. Poach halibut. (See below.)

4. Spread over hot or cold poached halibut steaks.

To Poach a Halibut:

1. Cover halibut with boiling salted water.

2. Add onion, lemon, and peppercorns.

3. Simmer, covered, for about 10 minutes for 1-inch thick steak. Add extra time for thicker steaks. When done, halibut will flake when tested with a fork.

4. Remove from heat. Keep in mind the halibut will continue to cook in a covered pan.

5. Serve hot or chill to serve cold.

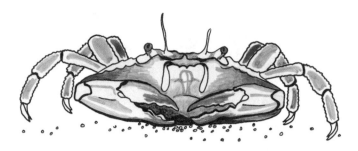

Crab Quiche

Contrary to popular fiction, real men will eat this quiche. In fact, get your share before they eat all of it.

1 pie crust
2½ cups crabmeat, pick out shell fragments
3 eggs
Juice of ½ lemon
Pinch of chili powder
1 cup cream
Salt and pepper to taste

1. Preheat oven to 375 degrees.

2. Bake the pie crust according to instructions.

3. Lightly beat the eggs and cream.

4. Add crab, lemon, chili powder, and seasonings.

5. Pour into pie shell.

6. Bake until the filling is firm and has browned, 25-35 minutes.

Zucchini Crab Cakes

Here's another way to enjoy all those blankety-blankety-blank zucchini. It takes about 1¼ pounds of crab legs to get 1½ cups of the meat. Shrimp meat can be substituted.

1 tablespoon oil
1 cup zucchini, coarsely shredded
¼ cup green onions, thinly sliced
1 egg, beaten
½ cup bread crumbs, fine dry
1 tablespoon Dijon-style mustard
½ teaspoon thyme
¼ teaspoon cayenne
1½ cups cooked crabmeat
½ cup sour cream
1 lemon or lime, sliced into wedges
⅛ teaspoon seasoned salt

1. In a large skillet heat one tablespoon cooking oil using medium high heat.

2. Cook zucchini and green onions until tender and liquid has evaporated, about 3 minutes.

3. Cool slightly.

4. In a large mixing bowl, combine beaten egg, bread crumbs, sour cream, mustard, thyme, and cayenne.

5. Add the zucchini mixture and crabmeat.

6. Mix well.

7. Make individual patties using about ¼ cup of the mixture.

8. Spray non-stick pan with cooking spray.

9. Using medium heat, fry for 3-4 minutes or until golden brown, turn once, and cook for another 3-4 minutes or until golden brown on both sides.

10. Sprinkle with seasoned salt, and serve with lemon or lime wedges.

Crab Mornay

A true "classic" that tastes so good it truly deserves the title.

1½ cups cooked crabmeat
1 cup fresh mushrooms, sliced
½ cup green onions, sliced
1 clove garlic, minced
2 tablespoons butter
2 tablespoons flour
Dash of white pepper
2 cups cream or milk
1 cup Swiss cheese, shredded
2 tablespoons dry sherry

1. In a medium saucepan sauté in butter over medium heat mushrooms, green onions, and garlic until tender.

2. Stir in flour and pepper.

3. Add cream all at once.

4. Stirring constantly, cook until sauce is thickened and bubbly.

5. Cook and stir for one minute more.

6. Reduce heat to low.

7. Add cheese to cream mixture; stir until melted.

8. Stir in crabmeat and dry sherry.

9. Heat through; do not boil.

10. Serve immediately over rice, biscuits, noodles, baked potatoes, or pastry shells.

Boiled Crab Dinner

Enjoy this Alaska version of the New England Lobster dinner.

---

2 lemons, quartered

½ cup cayenne

8 new red potatoes

½ cup white pepper

½ cup peppercorns

4 onions, peeled (Quarter large onions.)

6-8 Dungeness crabs

1 cup salt*

Two to four 12 oz. cans beer

Water

Be adventuresome and experiment with flavored salts.

1. Fill a large stockpot (at least 10 quarts) one-third full with water and beer.

2. Add lemons, potatoes, onions, salt, cayenne, white pepper, and peppercorns.

3. Cover and bring to a boil over high heat.

4. After ten minutes, add the crabs, cover, and return to boil.

5. Once steam begins to escape from under the lid, cook for 15-20 minutes.

6. Remove from heat and let sit, covered, for 10 minutes.

7. Serve with lots of beer and paper towels.

Ginger Apple Steelhead

My younger daughter calls this salmon apple pie. This is an excellent open fire recipe. Bury cooking packet in coals.

½ cup brown sugar

¼ cup corn oil

Juice of one lemon

¼ cup fresh ginger root, thinly sliced

2-3 tart green apples*, thinly sliced

2-3 lbs. steelhead fillets or salmon

*I prefer Granny Smith apples.

1. Combine brown sugar, oil, lemon juice, and ginger root.

2. Blend in blender starting at slowest speed and gradually increase speed until thoroughly blended. This takes 20-45 seconds. When done, you will have a fairly thick sauce.

3. Put a layer of apple slices on a large sheet of aluminum foil.

4. Place fish fillet, skin side down, on the apples.

5. Cover with half the sauce.

6. Layer apple slices over sauce-covered fillet.

7. Top with remaining sauce.

8. Fold foil over to make a cooking packet.

9. Using a second sheet of foil, encase the first cooking packet in a second foil cooking packet.

10. Bake for 20-30 minutes at 325 degrees on the middle rack of the oven.

Beer Batter #1

For years, my wife and I, with another couple, had an annual fish fry and potluck, inviting as many as two hundred people. We cooked the fish in cast-iron skillets over wood fires. Like all fish batters, this must be fried in hot oil or it will become soggy and laden with grease. Fry the fish a few pieces at a time. Firm meated white fish—halibut, cod, and salt water ling cod—are my favorites. This batter also produces great onion rings.

1 cup flour
1 teaspoon salt
¼ teaspoon pepper
1 tablespoon oil
2 eggs, separated
¾ cup beer*

*A great way to get rid of flat beer, or the beer you left in the back of the car when the temperature dropped to 20 below zero, and it froze. When you defrost frozen beer, remember to do it slowly or the cans will explode. I've also used this recipe to get rid of poor buying decisions when testing new brands.

1. Mix flour, salt, pepper, oil, and egg yolks.

2. Add beer and mix together.

3. Whip egg whites until stiff.

4. Fold egg whites into batter.

5. Dip fish and fry at 400 degrees.

Beer Batter #2

This is the quick and lazy man's way of making a beer batter. Actually, it is quite good and I've used it many times. Warning: thicker batters are more likely to hold grease than thin batters.

Pancake mix such as Bisquick
Beer

1. Mix together until you get a thin pancake batter consistency.

2. Dip fish and fry at 400 degrees.

3. Check the batter on the first piece of fish and if it is too thin, add a little more pancake mix.

4. If it is too thick, mix in more beer.

5. Serve warm.

Fish in Foil

Trout and grayling, fresh from the river, are a wonderful treat. I've also cooked whole salmon this way, increasing the bacon, onions, and so forth.

---

1 trout or grayling, 8-12 inches
1 slice bacon, cut in half
Salt and pepper
1 onion slice, one-half inch thick
1 lemon, sliced in ¼-inch pieces
1 pat of butter (Cooking spray OK.)
2 sheets aluminum foil

Cooking time will vary depending on size of fish and temperature of coals.

1. Spread butter on one sheet of aluminum foil.

2. Put trout on buttered foil.

3. Lightly salt and pepper the body cavity.

4. Put one piece of bacon, the onion slice, and lemon slices in the body cavity. You may need to cut onion slice into halves or quarters.

5. Top fish with remaining lemon slices and second piece of bacon.

6. Wrap tightly in foil.

7. Wrap packet in second sheet of foil.

8. Bury fish packet in coals of fire.

9. Cook 10-15 minutes*

10. Remove and eat.

Desserts and Sweets

P eople in the Far North crave the calories in sugars and fats to fight the cold. And this works, sometimes too well. Many of us insulate our bodies with too many extra calories requiring even larger clothing. We also have a collective sweet tooth.

Early sourdoughs survived prolonged periods with limited supplies, and they had to make do with what was available. But when supplies ran low, the three items they missed the most were tobacco, coffee, and sugar.

Sugar was universal. It flavored the bland and actuated the flavors of the Alaska's berries. Few fruit trees grow in the 49th State, but berries grow in every region. Salmonberries grow above pickers' heads in the more benign climate of the Panhandle and just above the ground along the Bering Sea. Berries turn hillsides and roadsides blue and red with at the ending of summer and beginning of fall. Bears, birds, and a host of other critters compete with humans for the bounty, but there is enough to share.

Homes often have a rhubarb plant or two for pie, syrup, or other sweets. Strawberries and rhubarb form a natural flavorful partnership and both grow profusely in the North. Alaskans also love ice cream, having one of the highest per-capita consumption rates in the nation. During the winter, we frequently leave it in the car or on the back porch until we're ready to eat it. When temperatures drop below minus 40, the ice cream is frozen so hard that it is almost impossible to scoop out. So we nuke it in the microwave. A series of 20-second bursts at 30 percent power works best. Too long at higher power melts spots inside the ice cream.

Ahkootuk or Akutaq

This is commonly known as Eskimo Ice Cream. Eskimos have as many variations as Italians have for spaghetti sauce. All are a combination of fish or meat fat (most commonly moose, reindeer, caribou, or seal oil) and blueberries, crowberries, huckleberries, and salmonberries. Some "modern" recipes substitute vegetable shortening such as Crisco and include sugar.

> 3-4 lbs. animal fat cut into very small pieces (or solid vegetable shortening)
> Water
> 1-2 cups berries
> Sugar to taste
> 1-2 cups fish or meat, cooked and shredded

1. Add a small amount of water to fat and whip until fluffy. As the fat absorbs water add more water in small amounts. Some recipes call for seal oil.

2. Whip the fat and water until fluffy and it cannot absorb more water. This can be done by hand, but an electric mixer makes the job a lot easier.

3. When fat is completely whipped, stir in the berries, meat or fish and sugar (start with ½ cup of sugar).

4. Add sugar gradually, tasting after each addition.

5. Thoroughly blend.

6. When finished, good Eskimo Ice Cream is smooth and light.

7. Serve. One popular way to serve is on pilot bread.

Note: Experienced cooks will see Eskimo Ice Cream as cake icing with meat or fish in it. Anyone who has made cake icing from scratch can make Eskimo Ice Cream.
I know one woman who now makes her Ahkootuk by mixing a can of pink cake icing with a can of tuna fish in oil. She whips the icing with a few tablespoons of water to fluff it up and blends in the tuna.

Baked Alaska

It is ironic that this recipe, which depends on fresh eggs, has Alaska in its name. Older eggs do not produce a frothy meringue, and historically most Alaska eggs came from the Lower 48. Before air freight became available, eggs frequently spent weeks, sometimes months, in transit and were decidedly "mature" by the time they reached Alaskans, particularly in Interior Alaska. "Cold Storage eggs," as they were known, had a distinctive taste. Some men who returned home after several seasons in the North found that fresh eggs tasted "peculiar." One year, the Yukon River froze early and a steamboat with a cargo of eggs could not make deliveries until the following spring. The winter's natural refrigeration preserved them.

½ gallon ice cream
One 9-inch sponge layer pound cake
6 large fresh egg whites
½ teaspoon cream of tartar
1 cup sugar

1. Put cake board or wooden cutting board into freezer.

2. Pack approximately 2 quarts of ice cream into an 8-inch diameter bowl.

3. Freeze until ready to serve.

4. Place the layer cake on cake board.

5. Refrigerate for at least 10 minutes.

6. When ready to serve, preheat oven to 500 degrees.

7. Beat egg whites with cream of tartar until frothy.

8. Gradually beat sugar in, continuing until meringue is stiff and glossy.

9. Place cake board or cutting board on a baking sheet.

10. Loosen ice cream and invert bowl over cake.

11. Remove bowl, completely cover cake and ice cream with meringue.

12. Spread meringue to board for a complete seal.

13. Place in oven and bake 3-5 minutes, or until meringue is lightly browned

14. Serve at once.

Blueberry Sauce

Adds flavor to cakes, ice cream and other sweets.

---

2 cups blueberries
½ cup water
2 cups sugar
1 teaspoon salt

1. Pick through the berries for twigs or leaves.

2. Mix blueberries in a saucepan with sugar, water, and salt.

3. Simmer until the berries have burst, approximately 10 minutes. Stir occasionally.

4. Remove from heat and cool.

5. Puree in a food processor.

6. Strain through a fine mesh strainer.

Blueberry Pie

Think of this as the apple pie of the north.

3 cups blueberries
1½ cups sugar
½ cup water for blueberries
2 tablespoons cornstarch
⅔ cup water for cornstarch
1 baked 9-inch pie shell
Ice cream or whipped cream (optional)

1. Mix blueberries, sugar, and ½ cup of water.

2. Bring to a boil and then reduce to a simmer.

3. Simmer gently until berries pop and make juice, about 10 minutes.

4. Stir cornstarch into ⅔ cup of water, removing all lumps.

5. SLOWLY stir cornstarch and water into berries.

6. Continue to simmer, stirring constantly, until cornstarch thickens, 3-8 minutes.

7. Pour into pie shell and chill for at least 30 minutes.

8. Top with whipped cream or ice cream before serving.

Cranberry Pie

This treat is not just for Thanksgiving. The cranberries may require more sugar, or less, depending on personal tastes. At step four, taste and incorporate more sugar if too tart

---

3 cups low bush cranberries (Commercial cranberries OK.)

1½ cups sugar (more or less)

1½ tablespoons cornstarch

¼ cup water

1 teaspoon vanilla extract

½ teaspoon salt

1 pie crust for two crust pie

1. Line pie plate with crust.

2. Combine cranberries, sugar, cornstarch, water, vanilla, and salt in a saucepan.

3. Bring to a slow boil, stirring occasionally.

4. When cornstarch has thickened, in 1-5 minutes, remove from heat.

5. Cool.

6. Pour filling into pie crust.

7. Put crust on top and cut three or more slits in crust.

8. Bake in preheated oven at 450 degrees for 10 minutes.

9. Reduce heat to 350 degrees and bake for another 30 minutes.

10. Remove from oven and allow to cool a bit before serving.

Dried Fruit Pie

This was a northern staple until relatively recently. Use any combinations of fruit or all of one kind. Because the sweetness varies so greatly with dried different fruits, the amount of sugar used will range greatly, from almost none to two cups.

4 cups water
3 cups dried fruit
½ to 2 cups sugar
2 tablespoons butter
¼ cup flour
1 pie crust, partially baked

1. Mix fruit and water.

2. Bring to a boil and then reduce to simmer.

3. Cook until fruit has absorbed almost all the water.

4. If the fruit is not fully reconstituted, add water ½ cup at a time.

5. When fruit is fully reconstituted, taste and stir in sugar, ½ cup at a time.

6. Stir in butter and flour.

7. Pour filling into pie crust.

8. Bake for 20-25 minutes in 350-degree oven.

Honey That Never Saw a Bee

(Also known as Fireweed Honey)

This is one of dozens of versions of this recipe, which was probably created originally by someone who missed real honey. For more intense flavor, add more flowers. But follow this recipe the first time and adjust for personal preferences the next time you make it.

---

10 cups sugar
2½ cups boiling water
1 teaspoon powdered alum
30 white clover blossoms
20 red clover blossoms
20 fireweed flowerets

1. Mix water, sugar, and alum.

2. Bring to rolling boil, let boil for 10 minutes.

3. Remove from heat.

4. Add flower blossoms (Use only the flower. Remove all stems).

5. Steep for 15 minutes.

6. Boil jar to sterilize in rolling boiling water bath.

7. Strain honey through cheese cloth into hot jars.

8. Place lid and bands immediately.

Rhubarb-Strawberry Pie

This is a natural northern combination.

---

1 to 2 cups sugar
3 tablespoons tapioca
½ teaspoon salt
¼ teaspoon powdered ginger
3 cups rhubarb, diced
2 cups strawberries, quartered
¼ cup water
¼ teaspoon grated lemon peel
One 9-inch pie crust plus top dough
1 tablespoon butter

1. Mix tapioca, sugar, salt, and ginger together.

2. Add fruit, lemon peel, water and thoroughly mix.

3. Let stand for 15-30 minutes.

4. Preheat oven to 400 degrees.

5. Pour fruit mixture into pie crust.

6. Chop butter into small pieces and sprinkle over top.

7. Make a lattice topping with extra dough on top of pie.

8. Bake for 35 minutes.

9. Allow pie to cool before cutting. It will thicken as it cools.

10. Serve, preferably with vanilla ice cream.

Alaskan Rhubarb & Strawberry Jam

Even with all the sugar, some people still might find it too tart.

2 lbs. rhubarb, chopped in 1-inch lengths
1½ cups water
1 to 2 cups strawberries
13 cups sugar (This not a typographical error!)
3 packages pectin, liquid

1. Simmer rhubarb in water until soft.

2. Add strawberries to make seven cups of berries and rhubarb.

3. Add sugar, bring to boil, stir constantly.

4. Boil for 1 minute.

5. Remove from heat.

6. Add pectin, and stir to blend thoroughly.

7. Pour into hot sterilized jars and seal.

8. Refrigerate until used.

Rosehip Pie

Rosehips are high in vitamin C. Unfortunately heat destroys most of the vitamin value when you cook them.

One 9-inch pie crust plus dough for top
1½ cup rose hips
1 stick butter, melted
1½ tablespoons cornstarch
1 cup sugar
2 eggs, slightly beaten
1 cup light corn syrup
2 lemons, juice only
½ teaspoon salt
1 teaspoon vanilla extract

1. Line pie plate with crust.

2. Core and remove the seeds from the rosehips.

3. Mix corn starch and sugar.

4. Blend in the melted butter.

5. Mix in the eggs, corn syrup, lemon juice, salt, and vanilla.

6. Stir in rose hips.

7. Pour filling into pie crust.

8. Top with either a lattice crust or full crust. If using a full crust, cut at least 3 slits.

9. Bake at 350 degrees for 35-45 minutes.

Salmonberry Pie

In Southeastern Alaska, where salmonberries are deep red, yellow, and light red, a combination of berries makes a pretty pie. For taste, I strongly prefer the flavor of the deep red berries with a few yellow ones for color.

---

6 cups salmonberries
1½ cups sugar
¼ cup cornstarch
¼ cup water
½ teaspoon salt
2 tablespoons butter
1 tablespoon lemon juice
One 9-inch pie crust plus dough for top

1. Combine cornstarch and water in bowl.

2. Whisk cornstarch and water together.

3. Stir in sugar, lemon juice, salt, and berries.

4. Stir to combine.

5. Pour into pie crust. Dot with small bits of butter.

6. Put top crust on and cut at least 3 slits in crust.

7. Bake on center rack of oven for 15 minutes at 450 degrees.

8. Reduce heat to 350 degrees and bake until brown, about 25-35 minutes.

About the Author

A writer, photographer, and teacher who knows his way around the kitchen, J. Stephen Lay in recent years has worked throughout North America, in Africa, in Australia, and in the Bahamas after living twenty-six years in Alaska, where, among other things, he edited food publications while at the Cooperative Extension Service at the University of Alaska Fairbanks.

Recommendations for readers interested in knowing more about Alaskans and how they live

ALASKA WOMEN WRITE
Living, Laughing, and Loving on the Last Frontier
edited by Dana Stabenow, paperback, $14.95

FASHION MEANS YOUR FUR HAT IS DEAD
A Guide to Good Manners and Social Survival in Alaska
by Mike Doogan, paperback, $14.95

GO FOR IT!
Finding Your Own Frontier
by Judith Kleinfeld, Ed.D., paperback, $14.95; hardbound, $22.95

IDITAROD DREAMS
A Year in the Life of Sled Dog Racer DeeDee Jonrowe
by Lew Freedman, paperback, $14.95

OUR ALASKA
Personal Stories about Life in the North
edited by Mike Doogan, paperback, $16.95

RAISING OURSELVES
A Gwitch'in Coming of Age Story from the Yukon River
Memoir by Velma Wallis, paperback, $14.95; hardbound, $19.95

TUNDRA TEACHER
Memoir by John Foley, paperback, $14.95

These and many other Alaska titles can be found at or special-ordered from your local bookstore, purchased directly from Epicenter Press by phoning the publisher's 24-hour toll-free order line, **800-950-6663,** or by visiting www.EpicenterPress.com. Orders may be mailed to: Epicenter Press, PO Box 82368, Kenmore, WA 98028. Visa, MC accepted. Add $4.95 for shipping. Washington residents add 8.7% sales tax.

EPICENTER PRESS
Alaska Book Adventures™
www.EpicenterPress.com